ACUPRESSURE FOR THE SOUL

How to Awaken
Biological Spirituality

and

The Gifts Of The Emotions

by

Nancy Fallon, PhD

Drawings by Michael Zane Tyree

The author is grateful for permission to use quotes
from Jane Robert's "Seth". Quotes are from a
variety of Jane's books and are indicated at the end
of each quote. Permission is granted in writing
from Robert Butts.

Drawings, cover design, and book design by
Michael Zane Tyree. Michael can be reached at
Light Technology Publishing, P.O. Box 1526,
Sedona, AZ 86339.

Library of Congress Catalog Card Number
93-086145
1. Transpersonal psychology 2. Biological Spirituality 3. Awakening the
Wonder Child 4. Chakras 5. Shiatsu 6. Shamanism 7. Title

ISBN 0-929385-49-7
Published by Light Technology Publishing
P.O. Box 1526, Sedona, AZ 86339

Printed by Mission Possible Commercial Printing
P.O. Box 1495, Sedona, AZ 86339

Acknowledgements

I thank the following people for impacting my life in the following ways:

Thank you Ohashi for pushing my buttons in order to activate my "yin" shiatsu abilities, and for the example of deepest respect for essence.

Thank you Dr. Marilyn Rossner for proving to me that we live beyond the grave:

"You're Aunt Anna (not her real name) is here," she said to me the first time we met. My Aunt Anna had died nine months previous to my meeting Marilyn.

And, thank you, Marilyn, for teaching me that our loving thoughts send healing to others without words ever being spoken:

"You were helping the dying man's wife," Marilyn whirled around to say to me in the middle of an M.D. friend's, and his wife's, story. The M.D. had attempted to resuscitate a stranger who had a heart attack at the restaurant where we were eating during a weekend workshop. While he and another doctor worked on the man, I kept feeling compassion for the dying man's wife and kept mentally saying to her, "It's not your fault." But, I never said anything out loud nor did I share that information with anyone.

Thank you Dan Gerber for giving me the opportunity to experientially learn that I am 100% responsible for my emotional reactions. Your offer of continued friendship after a profound disagreement touched me deeply. It was a turning point in my life. I feel eternally grateful for your brotherhood.

Dearest husband *Fred, thank you* for refusing to give up on me and my process; and for continuously supporting me, for five winters, to write this book.

A special thank you to the many clients, students, teachers, friends, and family who have touched me through the years by being who you are.

Dedicated

To
Jane Roberts, Robert Butts, and Seth

Jane is one of the greatest natural mystics of our times. When asked to define mysticism Jane wrote,

> *To me it's a sort of...yes, sturdy connection of one person to the universe...a one-to-one relationship; a yearning to participate in the meaning of existence; a drive to appreciate nature and salute it while adding to it; but the knowledge that nature is also a touchstone to a deeper unknowable essence from which we and the world spring. (Unknown Reality, Volume One,* by Jane Roberts, Appendix 1).

Seth describes himself as an entity no longer focused in physical reality. For twenty one years he spoke and wrote books through Jane.

"*You create your own reality,*" Seth said many times and in many ways. "*You are in physical existence to learn and understand that your energy, translated into feelings, thoughts and emotions, causes all experience. There are no exceptions.*" (Session 614, September 13, 1972, 11:25pm, *The Nature Of Personal Reality.*)

Robert Butts took dictation, by hand, from Seth for over 20 years. And, he did the notes at the end of each session which often entailed researching current pertinent information in order to give the reader as much background as possible.

"Value fulfillment..." "Greatness..." "Natural state of grace..." these come to mind to describe what Jane, Rob and Seth exemplify for me.

This book is based on these beliefs:

✤ What we believe is true in life is what we get to experience. As we change our beliefs so do our experiences change. Therefore, there is no one universal truth, but as many truths as there are thoughts and feelings.

✤ Everything comes into physical being through the feminine aspect, which is form, and is naturally Good: the Goddess (form) and God (spirit) made One.

✤ For over 2,000 years, as a species, we have chosen to experience polarities: upper-lower, good-bad, yin-yang, emotions-intellect, dark-light, spirit-form, metaphysical senses-physical senses, and death-birth. Polarities are parts of a whole.

✤ The opportunity has arrived for our planet to operate out of wholeness. The emotions and the intellect, spirit and form, religion and science, metaphysical senses and physical senses, yin and yang, can become One again in a state of cooperation and love...if we so choose.

*"Do not place the words of gurus,
ministers, priest, scientists, psychologists, friends
– or my words – higher than the feeling
of your own being."*

The Nature of Personal Reality,
Seth Session 677, July 11, 1973, 10:01 pm

Contents:

"*You are born loving. You are born
compassionate. You are born curious about yourself
and your world. Those attributes also belong to natural law.
You are born knowing that you possess a unique, intimate
sense of being that is itself, and that seeks its own fulfillment,
and the fulfillment of others. You are born seeking the
actualization of the ideal. You are born seeking to add value
to the quality of life, to add characteristics, energies, abilities
to life that only you can individually contribute to the world,
and to attain a state of being that is uniquely yours,
while adding to the value fulfillment
of the world.*"

— Seth
The Individual And The Nature Of Mass Events,
Session 862, June 25, 1979

Introduction

As a species, we can no longer afford to repress emotions, label them as "bad", and relegate them to being less desirable than "logic." The results of doing the aforementioned, these past 3-5,000 years, has been –

1) the abuse of children: they represent emotions uncontrolled,

2) the rape and pornogrifying of women: women are, archetypically, the embodiment of emotion,

3) the mutilation of other species: if one does not "feel" then one can violate the spirit and body of other species, and very sadly, logically justify it,

4) the near destruction of Planet Earth–the Earth is considered female, the substance form of God/Goddess/All-That-Is, i.e., our "feeling" self made flesh. The color of dark skinned women especially archetypically symbolizes the loam, womb of our spirit in physical form, the Great Mother Goddess of us all.

What children, women, Mother Earth, and the animals all have in common is the ability to naturally and easily emote. Because of women's ability to give birth—a very emotional event—and her built in ability to nurture, woman is the embodiment of emotion. Emotions and how to feel them and how to use them are her gift to humankind. Men have these same gifts of emoting and figuratively birthing, which are a part of their yin aspect. They are activated when men are being emotionally/spiritually nurturing and creative.[1]

The animals, and their natural displays of emotion, were highly aligned with the feminine in the days of the Goddess religions, when our species lived more directly connected to Mother Earth. As our mass consciousness focused more on the intellect, Patriarchal religions, and industrialization, our mass consciousness began to disconnect from the animals and the direct connection with Nature that they represented.

As a result we swung the pendulum too far to the right and began to devalue people that weren't white, male and Christian.[2] In this patriarchal system "white male" represents the ultimate in awakened-crown-chakra, enlightened-logical-intellect, and is in direct contrast to Great Black Earth Mother. Over the centuries this has caused the mass consciousness of the human species to desperately long for the reunion of its "Black Earth Goddess" self (emotions) with its "White Male God" (intellect) counterpart.

The purpose of this book is to focus on healing and reunion between Mother Earth and Father Sky. Let's imagine what it would be like if each human lived and believed, that animals, plants, and Mother Earth were just as sacred and capable of cooperative love as humans are. Imagine that every being and every object on Planet Earth was God, Goddess, All That Is, incarnate. Imagine the life of a fly being as sacred as your own. What thoughts and feelings come up for you? What beliefs in particular come into question? Are you able to imagine the fly as sacred as you are?

Since childhood I have believed that all life forms are sacred. To me the respect shown between various animal species, even between predator and prey, is trying to show humans how inter-connected we all are. To manifest this inter-species homeostatic state of natural grace to include humans, we have to resurrect the beauty and the power of the emotions. For it is on the emotional plane that we can empathically relate to the sacredness of other species and form.

To reach this experience, we have to *live* that emotions are *equal* in importance to thoughts and logic. Many of you may find this dogmatic and a very strong stand. And for me it is. Currently, human beings and domesticated animals trained to do so, are the only beings that I know of that torture and mutilate each other and other species.[3] A hungry predator punctures the jugular vein, or punctures the "take out" acupuncture point in the hamstring in order to bring down its prey for the kill. That is not torture. Domesticated cats remember this skill but don't really need it anymore. Thus, they appear to be "torturing" their prey. But, watch a hungry alley cat. She does not "toy" this way very long.

Seth explains this deep biologically spiritual understanding between predator and prey:

> *"Animals have a sense of justice that you do not under-stand, and built-in to that innocent sense of integrity there is biological compassion, understood at the deepest cellular levels...A cat playfully killing a mouse and eating it is not evil. It suffers no guilt. On biological levels both animals understand."*[4]

If you are having a strong emotional reaction to this informa-tion then know that you are on the verge of benefiting from your emotions. You are being offered an opportunity to explore and learn what your feelings are trying to tell you.

I am not making you feel what you are feeling. Only you and your own beliefs can make you feel. I hope you will take the opportunity to own your feelings and to benefit from them, for this is what this book is about.

Part I introduces the idea of biological spirituality. When I was a child studying the Nitrogen Life Cycle I had my first gut level realization of what the life-death-rebirth system in Nature and in the changing of the seasons was trying to show humans. The following timely tragedy piqued my curiosity about this inevitable life/death cycle that all physical beings, without exception, will someday experience:

> *"One February morning, just before my 13th birthday, my beautiful Collie dog was struck by a car and killed. In the dead of Winter I asked my father to get out the tractor and to carry my "King" Collie dog on the stone bolt back to our old farm and to place King under the walnut tree half way up the mountain. We couldn't bury him because the ground was frozen. As I think back what a kind father I had, because he did even though he had to put chains on our Farmall H tractor in order to get through the deep Vermont snow.*
>
> *Afterward, I weekly made a trip up to the old Walnut tree to see how King was doing. I was so awed by Mother Nature's process of decomposition that I had a mystical revelation that there really was no death, only transformation. In the early summer, one and one half years later, all that was left was a few hairs. And up through the hairs a bunch of wild violets was growing!"*

It was then clear to me that Mother Nature was daily, seasonally, and constantly showing us that death is rebirth. Part I describes the human consciousness components of this life-death-rebirth cycle that attempts to continuously show the human species that we are indeed biologically spiritual.

Chapter One introduces the connection of the emotions with the chakra system as it was in the days of the Goddess religions. Teachings from Oriental medicine further indicates the connection of our emotions with the feminine, the childself, the animals, the seasons, and Mother Earth.

Chapter Two shows the intricately entwined world of emotions with the cycle of the seasons, and our cycles as human beings when we are aware that we are biologically spiritual.

Chapter Three points out that in order to open up to a new way of living, a part of us has to die. This is Mother Nature's law of life-death-rebirth. The seasons teach us this, the cycle of each physical life on this planet constantly shows us this. But, humans are so disconnected from their biological spirituality that they fear this life-death-rebirth cycle so much that they, in fact, are often living "frozen-in-fear" lives. This chapter shows us that to die is to be reborn.

After we are reborn, a miracle happens, we have a renewed zest for living. Chapter Four describes this zest for living in terms of becoming "self-actualized," "following one's bliss," and pursuing a living doing what one loves or to enjoy what one is currently doing. People who have accomplished this are called ordinary monks and mystics, by Marsha Sinetar.[5] Seth describes this as value fulfillment. Value fulfillment may mean living this lifetime in bliss, or experiencing, in depth, some specific focus, such as what it's like to be blind, or mentally impaired. This aspect of value fulfillment is not covered in this book. The aspect I am focusing on is the development of the values of learning to become emotional beings and the transformations involved when a person first allows him or herself to feel the feelings s/he is carrying around in his and her body.

Part II describes the benefits of feeling emotions and offers ways of how the power of each emotion can be beneficially used on a daily basis to enhance all aspects of one's life. Once the barn full of repressed emotional caeca is cleaned out, then one can more easily experience the benefit of the gentle breeze of emotions constantly blowing through the sweet grass in the hay mow. Often beliefs that emotions are bad, something to get rid of and/or are the work of the devil have to be addressed. Mental exercises to help the reader move through these beliefs are included in each of the chapters 7-11.

Chapter Five, The Gifts of the Emotions, outlines each emotion and what it's power is. To view and experience emotions as positive and essential powers in our lives we, as a species, need to be re-educated about their beauty and purpose. Re-educating over 3,000 years of denial isn't going to happen over night. Much compassion and patience is needed for yourself and others in this undertaking. Thinking in terms of all of us being children in the learning and developing of these emotional powers has helped me awaken the kind of compassion and understanding needed.

I was delighted when the Healing of the Inner Child movement came into being. My own work was hinting at it when I began the Magical Childself workshops back in 1985. I soon switched to the current healing the inner child language because it is so universal. Everyone was once a child and so we, no matter what culture or part of the Globe we are from, have a common ground from which to work.

Chapters Six through Ten go into depth how to awaken the Wonder of each of the five emotions: fear, anger, compassion, sadness, and grief are the terms used in this book to describe and categorize the various emotions. Each emotion is presented with the underlying theme that each feeling is LOVE in its various forms. We would not feel any of the emotions if we did not love. We cannot fully love if we are not feeling our emotions.

While I was healing my own inner child I was also studying Zen style shiatsu, a form of very reverent acupressure that includes heavy grounding in Traditional Chinese Medicine. I already had several years experience in teaching and counseling. And as I began to do deep spiritual type bodywork with my clients, many would begin to remember physical, sexual and emotional abuse as far back as conception. Conceptional type abuse is often in the form of sensing that one was not a "wanted" baby.

From these clients I began to realize that one of the most wounded groups of people currently on this Planet falls under the category of "Infant" using the Healing the Inner Child terms. Any person born who was not wanted by at least one significant other, has been, to some degree, emotionally wounded. Most Healing-the-Inner-Child therapists agree that all of us have been, at one time or another, emotionally wounded because of how our culture is set up. Those of us wounded in infancy, prior to the crawling and verbal stages in our lives, experience this wound on an unconscious and very deep cellularly encoded level.

Cellularly encoded means that the chemistry of each cell in our bodies has been disturbed by this very early emotional, usually unconscious and unintentional, abuse. Being emotionally "not wanted" by either parent, or a significant other, at this early stage most often results in some form of oral addiction. I define infancy as beginning at conception and continuing through the first nine months of physical life.

During this "I am you" stage of development the child and parents are in constant telepathic communication. The more conscious the parents are of this communication, the better they can convey their wishes and intentions to the unborn child, and the more informed of a choice the child can make as to whether to be born or not.

As authentic Spirit world communicators know, no child ever really dies. Children can grow up just as happy in spirit world, and often happier, than on the physical plane. In animal species and early in the Goddess religions when humans still lived closely connected with the life-death cycles of Nature, it was often decided, out of love, to not bring the young into this world. Or, quite often, the young were killed immediately after being born because the mother knew the conditions were not right for a *quality* of life for her new born, and that the infant's focus wasn't fully physical yet.

In the wild animal world this practice continues today. To humans this behavior is not acceptable. Because of our ability to "reflect" on the past we have the opportunity to develop ways to insure that everyone has a quality life by learning ways to lovingly birth children into spirit world, or better yet, to become so conscious that the decision is made mutually before the child is born—preferably before conception.

Even after conception conscious conversation with the unborn can result in a wise unborn child choosing to go back to Spirit World and for all involved to have a more loving quality of life. The pioneering research of Dr. Gladys McGarrey, M.D. proves this conversation to be possible. Dr. McGarrey uses dreams, visualization and letter writing techniques for mothers to communicate with their unborn children. If a woman wants an abortion Dr. McGarrey suggests first communicating this to her unborn child in one of the mentioned methods. Quite often, she reports, the child will naturally abort itself.

Dr. McCarrey further reports that one mother who had an abortion later decided to have a child. When the child was about three she casually told her mother that she had come once before but that Mom wasn't ready so she had contentedly gone back into Spirit World.[6]

Because the majority of our species does not believe in a spirit life equal in importance to this physical one, and because we have disconnected from incorporating that spirit life into the physical one, i.e., biological spirituality, we have not yet developed a consciousness that takes full responsibility for a *quality* of life of all beings. Instead we continue to focus on saving every physical human life, often ignoring the dignity of the human desiring a quality life—and, we unconsciously continue to destroy other species lives, and their habitats out of a deep fear that if we don't have a physical life, then we don't have a life.

Since Mother Nature is always seeking balance, it is no accident that many people globally are experiencing "crash" courses in learning about Spirit World.[7] These crash courses are being experienced in the form of near death experiences; disassociation skills learned to survive physical, sexual and emotional abuse; and, unexplained spiritual experiences due to the death of a loved one, a severe accident, life threatening illness, or high fever.[8] Infants are experiencing them, as well as children and adults. Many do not realize that they are learning about Spirit World for they are told it's just their imagination. And many others keep quiet for years about their experiences because they never hear anyone else talking about such experiences. But, the high percentage of people beginning to communicate these experiences is changing all this.

As I listened to other people's stories I realized that since I was a young child I have been communicating with spirits. I believe we all *naturally* do, then it is educated out of us. The imaginary playmate is quite often a loving friend from spirit world. My playmate was my deceased sister. Her toy chest was in my bedroom. She had died at age seven. Seven years later I was born. My parents never healed from the tragedy of her death, and even though I was considered to be my sister reincarnated, my mother was afraid to love me for fear she would lose me again. Thus, even though my mother was physically present, I felt abandoned, insecure, and tried to die several times.

Now I know I chose those circumstances and now have a very loving relationship with my mother even though she is in spirit world. The skills of spirit world communication, and communication with cellularly encoded memories is invaluable in my work today.

During this early childhood development period, my father was the nurturer. He loved me unconditionally. Because he and Mom never healed the pain between them, Dad and I grew emotionally co-dependent. Consequently I grew up believing Dad was a god. He *was* my first spiritual teacher. He gave me an appreciation for nature, wild animals, and first hand contact with the teachings of farm animals. I loved every minute of it.

Mom loved Nature as well. She was more academic about it. She could name every bird that came to her many bird feeders. She pressed and labeled the wild flowers of Vermont. She had an extensive collection of mounted butterflies. She taught Nature at summer camps as well as being a full time public school teacher.

The gifts both my parents gave could be material for yet another book. I have synthesized those gifts into healing the child within via acupressure. I call it Shin Shiatsu based on my training in Zen style shiatsu. This book is the outcome of years of study combining counseling, bodywork, Oriental medicine, and formal training in spirit world communication. From these many years of study I concluded that it is our emotions and passion-for-living-a-quality-life, or lack of them, that powers the creations of our imaginations. It is through our imaginations and emotions that we co-create our world.

The final chapter asks the reader to imagine what his or her life would be like if each human's ideal world vision came true. How would you like the world to be? Each person's reality begins with a vision. Emotions are the power that manifest that vision. When enough pain from the past, and perhaps the future, are healed, a person becomes free again to feel creative, to imagine greatness, and to follow his or her bliss in life. Just imagine.

Introduction Notes

1. In Oriental teachings "yin" is the term used to define the feminine half of All-That-Is. Yang defines the masculine half of All-That-Is. And there is some yin in every yang aspect as well as yang in every yin aspect. This is a very surface definition for the purpose of giving the reader a concept of yin and yang.

2. It appears that this was a political, though perhaps an unconscious, decision of the mass consciousness of the human species. Of note is the fact that after about 28,000 years of worshiping the Great Mother, the following great male teachers were born within a 1000 year span: Buddah born 560 BC, Confucius born 551 BC, Jesus born about 4 BC and Muhammad born about 570 AD

3. When living conditions grow poor animals will also kill their own species in order to preserve a quality of life. This is often mistaken as just a "survival of the fittest" behavior. We discredit them and our own intelligence by such a limited concept.

4. Roberts, Jane, *Nature of Personal Reality*, Seth session 634.

5. The term "self-actualized" is from Abraham Maslow. The idea of following one's bliss is Joseph Campbell's. The concept of ordinary people as monks and mystics is Marsha Sinetar's; she also has a book titled, *Ordinary People as Monks and Mystics*.

6. This information is taken from a speech Dr. Gladys McGarrey, M.D. gave at the International Institute of Integral Human Sciences and Spiritual Science Fellowship in Montreal, Quebec, Canada, in May of 1992. Speech title: "Contacting the Physician Within."

7. "Spirit world" is a term used by the Spiritualist Church and mediums who do "spirit world" communication. It usually refers to the deceased, although some entities who claim to having never been physical may also communicate to mediums and especially "channels". To look up the scientific research done on spirit world communication and mediumship, I refer you to three books edited by Brian Ingllis: (1) *Mediumship and Survival*, (2) *Hauntings and Apparitions, An Investigation of the Evidence*, (3) *Through the Time Barrier*. Also, the book *Channeling*, by John Klimo, offers excellent explanations of channeling and spirit world communication.

8. These are all documented ways people are learning to identify their existence beyond the physical. For information about the extensive research done on near death experiences look up *Heading Toward Omega*, and *Life At Death*, by Kenneth Ring. Dr. Raymond Moody, the pioneer in this research, is a teacher at large for the International institute of Integral Human Sciences, Montreal Quebec. I highly recommend his books, *Life After Life*, and *Reflections on Life After Life*.

1

The Sacred Void Of Passage

The Awakening of the Chakras

I am the spiraling spirant that spiritualizes spirit into form. I am the DNA and the RNA that caduceus in your spinal cord. I am the coiled serpent waiting at your coccyx to become the Life Force Goddess known as "kundalini." I am alive long before you are born and I pulsate throughout your many lives making it look like you die and are reborn again, and again, even in this life time. I am the Alpha and the Omega and yet I have no beginning and no end. I am the endless circle of electrons and protons and in Nature I show myself as spirals. The spirals represent the unfathomable LoveSpirit that breathes the Life Force into your energy vortices called Chakras.

Affirmation:
I feel the love of God/Goddess/All-That-Is spiraling upward through my head, and downward through my feet. The spiral gets bigger and bigger until I am buoyed in spiraling spirit and I feel loved.

The Sacred Void Of Passage

The Awakening of the Chakras

To an extent, some people in the
sciences manage to blend the so-called female and
male characteristics. When they do so, seeming oppositions
and contradictions disappear. To whatever degree, more than
their contemporaries, they do not allow sexual roles to blind
them psychologically. Therefore, they are more apt to combine
reason and emotions, intuitions and intellect, and in so doing
invent theories that reconcile previous contradictions. They
unify, expand, and create, rather than diversify.
Einstein was such a person in the sciences.

— Seth
The Nature of the Psyche: Its Human Expression Session 772, April 19, 1976

In the beginning is the womb, the sacred nurturing darkness in which we all grow. "O-o-o-o-m-m-m," a mother births a child into being, a cow gives birth to her calf and mammalian mothers everywhere make the universal sound of "om" as they bring a life through the sacred void of passage represented by their birth canal. There is nothing in the world more activating of the first, second, and third chakras than natural birthing, nurturing the newborn and personally having the power to co-create a new life either in essence or in form. The moans and groans of birth "om" a being from a focus of suspension between spirit and form into physical life. This creation process is true whether one is birthing a new being, or a new idea. And, it is our first three chakras that carry the essence and power of any creation process.[1]

The *root chakra* located where the penis and vagina/clitoris are, represents the location of our most basic physical needs for warmth, food and touch, which translate into a sense of being unconditionally loved when this kind of physical touch is given to us lovingly.[2]

In women it is also the location of the entrance of a child into this world. In a man it is the location of the tunnel in the penis through which the seeds for a new life pass. The vagina and the man's urethra are sacred voids of passage of life from one form to another.[3]

It is the feminine in all of nature that provides the sacred void. It is the masculine that provides the seeds. The two are partners and parts of the human holographic picture. Each contains a dotted line blue print for the other in his and her genes. Yet, it is the feminine that is the giver of all life. For the first two months in the uterus all mammals, including humans, are female.

The feminine energy is stronger, can endure longer, and so can "hold a space" during the first two crucial months of establishing new life in a womb.[4] Sjoo and Mor report the fact that,

> *"The vulnerability of the male newcomer within the female environment is well known. Vaginal secretions are more destructive to the Y bearing sperm. The mortality rate is higher among neonate and infant males. Within the womb, the male fetus, for the first two months, is protected by being virtually indistinguishable from a female."*[5]

It is the blood of woman that gives life to man and her species. It is the second energy center in both men and women that harbors this nurturing, compassionate memory of our oneness with each other and with All-That-Is.

In humans there are two accepted locations for the womb or *spleen center.*[6] In Oriental medicine, the spleen is analogous to the pancreas, in particular, the hormones used in the female reproductive system. In the Law of the Five Elements, the stomach and spleen meridians make up the Element Earth. Both meridians are highly connected with the reproductive system and the stomach meridian travels directly through the nipples–the very source of sustenance and life for a new born baby.[7]

The name spleen chakra, when viewed through Oriental teachings, points heavily toward a strong feminine, emotional, relationship whether it is located in the womb/prostate area, or in the left ovary/stomach area.

Oriental teachings further show us that each man has a feminine aspect (Yin) and each woman carries a masculine aspect (Yang). When a person's male and female aspects are balanced, the person's intellect and emotions are equal and work harmoniously together. However, most humans no matter what race they are from, do not have their first and second chakras awakened. In fact they receive many messages to do the contrary especially in the Patriarchal religions. Now this is being carried over into the New Age teachings that emphasize repression or control of the first two energy centers while emphasizing development of centers four through seven.

The *Third Chakra*, the solar plexus, is the focus of development in Buddhism and comes close to incorporating the intuitive "gut level" instincts often assigned as a feminine trait, yet it too neglects the importance of centers one and two.[8]

This third center, called the *Power Center*, like the second center, has two possible locations. One is in the solar plexus area with the liver to the back and to the right of it. The other is near the navel which brings the intellectual abilities into closer alignment with the intuitive "gut level" abilities. If, however, the second center is not awakened and healthy then a person may be intellectually loving, i.e., is in service to humanity out of "should's, have-to's, and rules and regulations", but not necessarily emotionally balanced. Nor will s/he usually be in harmony with his or her feminine, nurturing, receptive, passive, or emotionally based sexual aspects. The **Emotional Energy Development Chart** on the next two pages displays the links among the Five Elements, energy centers, meridians, and emotional functions.

E M O T I O N A L E N E R G Y				
AGE	**EMOTION/ FUNCTION**	**CHAKRA**	**ELEMENT**	**MERIDIANS**
Infancy (I am you) conception to 9 months	Fear/ Courage to Change	Root	Water	Bladder & Kidney
Pretoddler (I am you & me) 9 mos. to 18 mos.	Compassion/ Balance of Boundaries	Womb	Earth	Stomach & Spleen
Toddler (I am me) 18 mos. to 3 years	Anger/ the Power To Be	Power	Wood	Liver & Gall Bladder
Preschool (Independent stage) 3 to 6 yrs.	Joy and Sadness	Heart	Fire	Heart, Small Intestine Pericardium Sanjiao
School Age (Interdependent age) 7 to 12 yrs.	Grief/ the Wisdom to Trust	Throat	Metal	Lung & Large Intestine
Adolescence 12 to 18 Yrs.	Respect for Differences	Third Eye	The yin aspects of all	conception Vessel
Adult (Self actualization)	Reverence	Crown	The yang aspects of all	Governing Vessel

D E V E L O P M E N T	C H A R T
ADULT FUNCTION EFFECTED	**SOURCES FOR HEALING**
Sense of security, sense of being loved unconditionally	• Warm to Hot Baths • Nurturing bodywork • Listen to lullabies • Play-act a happy infant • Have a loved one feed and bathe you
Emotional boundaries between Self, childself, other humans and other species	• Sacred sweat lodges • Drumming • Play with a puppy of kitten, one year old child or adult you feel safe with
Sense of Self/Soul worth to fulfill purpose in life	• Practice honoring your likes and dislikes • Learn to say No and not feel guilty • Chanting • Ha breath
Sense of Self in relation to others. Harmony between the intellect and the emotions	• Singing • Laughing with others • Spend time daily asking what your child self is feeling • Practice being curious
Communication skills, clear listening and clear expressing capabilities	• Practice cooperative adventures • Do grieving ceremonies • Say goodbye to the critical parent inside you
Perception and reception abilities in general which are directly dependent on the level of emotional functioning of the first three chakras	• Heal the first three chakras
The ability to bring the polarities into Oneness. The ability to feel and know the awe and wonder in Self and All-That-Is	• Develop the abilities of chakras 1 through 5

Healthily woven together in a web of swirling human electricity, the first three energy centers represent: physical needs *(root center)*, in harmony with the emotions *(womb center)*, in balance with a sense of personal self-worth *(power center)*. A person balanced in centers one, two, and three lives by two natural laws:

the law of loving self-acceptance

the law of cooperation = *Healthy Compassion*

These two natural laws are, in fact, instinctive and innate desires among all cells and all species of consciousness. "Loving self-acceptance" reflects a natural state of grace. In order to lovingly accept the differences and preferences of "other," one has to be able to lovingly accept and love all aspects of one's self. In other words, to unconditionally love one's self. We cannot unconditionally love "others" and All-That-Is until we do. When we are in a state of unconditionally loving our selves then we exude the essence of being in a natural state of grace. Without cell cooperation we would not have organs or bodies. Without cooperation from other species of consciousness, such as plants, we would not have food to eat. Life isn't a matter of survival of the fittest, it is a cooperation among species to maintain *quality* of physical life.

Human beings, because of our over emphasis on the intellectual polarity for over 2,000 years, have distorted our innate sense of balance in Nature to the brink of destruction. Since the laws of loving self-acceptance and cooperation are so biologically encoded in All-That-Is in physical form, we have social movements going on globally to reawaken those innate abilities to love self and others unconditionally and to have cooperation among ourselves and other species. Movements such as Perestroika, Glassnost, Greenpeace, feminism, and the demand for rights of gays and lesbians, to name but a few, all reflect a mass need of humans to be lovingly accepted, respected, and to have full freedom to live cooperatively with all other beings on Earth at this time. Granted, the pains of individuals distort the actions of these movements at times, but the innate need for loving self acceptance and interspecies cooperation is the basis for these movements.

Unconditional love and cooperation are a function of energy centers one, two, and three being equally healthy. On a mass scale they are currently very unhealthy resulting in much blood being shed and many distortions occurring.

The distortions such as child abuse, abuse of feminine aspects in all of Nature, substance and process addictions, psychosomatic illness, religious dogmatism, and playing life and death games such as war, all reflect unbalanced first, second, and third energy centers, not only in individuals, but in communities and nations. These distortions further reflect over 3,000 years of masses of people learning to deny and repress emotions, the feminine and the child-within.

There are timely movements going on in seminars and therapies that teach individuals to "heal the child within", and to reconnect, via the wonder child self, to our biologically spiritual self. Many Native American teachings, Father Matthew Fox's "Creation Centered Spirituality," and Joseph Campbell's, Power of Myth, teach us links between our feminine and naturally biological spirituality. Shin Shiatsu and Iona Teeguarden's Jin Shin Do, are two body therapies that I am familiar with that connect the inner child self, a balanced masculine and feminine self, and the spiritual self, with the physical body.

Teachers and examples of whole being can also be found in core near-death-experiencers who have made peace with themselves, and in Abraham Maslow's "self-actualized" people, and Marsha Sintar's "ordinary people as monks and mystics." Many others who are actively healing the child within are also examples to us by there very being. This does not mean that these people stop having feelings. On the contrary. They feel more, and more frequently.

Some of them are inmates in our mental institutions. The late Itzac Bentov (quantum physicist) made the statement that a preview of our future selves can be seen in the abilities of people in our mental institutions: "*...possibly 25 to 30 percent of all institutionalized schizophrenics belong to this category—a tremendous waste of human potential.*"[9]

For centuries being "emotional" has been equated with being "crazy" and usually assigned to be a female trait. As a species, we are beginning to heal that thousands-of-years-old misconception. The coming forward of so many women and men abused in their childhood years, a media that provides immediate mass communication, and a common language, "healing of the inner child", that therapists, lay people, and all cultures can understand, forecasts a global transformation in a relatively short period of time.

We, as humans, are so longing for our natural inheritance—union with All-That-Is—that we are globally creating ways to throw ourselves into awakening processes tailored for both the individual and large groups of people. Near death experiences, religious wars, being part of natural disasters, participating in incurable diseases (either as host or helper), and spiritual dramas of all kinds are our species attempts to reunite with our natural inheritance: biological spirituality.

Biological Spirituality is more easily described than defined. In essence, every single cell in physical existence is encoded with a sense of purpose, dignity, and divinity. Every cell in existence is God, Goddess, All-That-Is, made physical. Every plant, mineral, insect, animal, and human being is innately divine. This is not a new concept. Many spiritual practices at many different times and in many different ways have espoused this idea. The point is that, on a mass scale we are moving toward acknowledging and living our biological spirituality. And, it is in the reawakening of child-like wonder in each of us that we can learn to reconnect with the divinity that has always been All-That-Is.

Part of awakening to our bio-spirituality is acknowledging all physical functions to be divine acts: birthing, eating, sleeping, defecating, urinating, sex, bathing, and dying. It means reconnecting with the emotions, the weather, the seasons, all of Mother Natures rhythms and what She is constantly teaching us through them about our biological spirituality. It is no coincidence that during the past 20 years natural foods, natural therapies, and the exercise craze have been booming. It is part of the reconnecting with our bio-spiritual selves that is globally taking place. Healing of the inner child, healing from child abuse, spouse abuse, addictions, racial and sexual prejudices, and healing the environment of Mother Earth are all aspects of reclaiming our biological right to divinity.

Spiritually, the fastest growing forms of expression are ones that connect hands-on healing, the feminine, and closeness to Mother Earth. All of which are functionally related to the development of the first three energy centers, i.e., our physical needs, our emotional/womb aspects, and our personal power abilities to Be who we are. During the last 20 years, the unearthing of messages left to us by the Goddess religions kindled the resurgence of the feminine and sexual aspect of spirituality. Merlin Stone's book, *When God Was A Woman*, along with others, awakened the feminine in both men and women to the importance in becoming bio-spiritual once again.[10]

Soon afterward, the teachings of shamanism resurfaced reacquainting us with our connections to animals, sacred vaginas into the womb of Mother Earth, called "journeys into the under world," and how to travel there to find a totem animal or bird, i.e., a symbol of biological spirituality. The resurgence of Tantric yoga, teaching sex as divine, is currently sweeping the country in New Age circles.

All of these ways of reconnecting with biological spirituality are a result of global cellular urgings toward wholeness and union that have become too great to ignore. The balancing of the physical with the emotional with the spiritual with the mental is occurring in all aspects of physical beingness. We are all contributing by being a member of Planet Earth at this time. How we each contribute is an individual choice.

Some of us will have easy births into reclaiming our biological spirituality. Some of us will suffer greatly and yet, that suffering can be great teachers to each of us, as we embark on this inevitable journey. The birth canal into biological spirituality is spiraled with the natural cycles. We begin with the climate and the seasons of the emotions.

Chapter One Notes

1. Much has been written about the chakra system in our bodies. Chakra is a sanskrit word meaning energy vortex. I highly recommend the book, *Energies Of Transformation*, by Bonnie Greenwell, PhD., and the studies done by Japanese parapsychologist, Dr. Hiroshi Motoyama in his book, *Theories Of The Chakras: Bridge To Higher Consciousness*. Dr. Motoyama, a research psychologist in Japan, invented a devise called the AMI machine to measure the energy vortexes. This devise measures skin currents and can detect electric, magnetic and optical changes in a person's energy vortexes.

The experience of the chakras is an emotional one, and involves a commotion of energy called "kundalini, which is also a sanskrit word. My experiences are documented in the corresponding chakra notes.

2. In 1983 I began consciously studying spirituality. One of my teachers was Mitra, a man trained in the Jain monk tradition who focused on the awakening of the chakras. Each time I would take a week end workshop with him, I would have a "chakra-awakening experience." The process took about six years and led me into the importance of healing the inner child.

My interpretation of these experiences, plus my knowledge of Traditional Oriental Medicine led to the description of the functions of the chakras presented in this book.

Mitra is now deceased. He died of AIDS in 1987.

3. At the time this chakra awakened Mitra confirmed that my second, sixth and seventh chakras were already functioning. (I personally believe we expand them and contract them like an oscillating orifice with our beliefs about them.)

My first and second energy vortexes experienced explosions of white light that felt like they were each a ball about seven inches in diameter. I did not know anything about the involvement of the emotions when such phenomena occurs until in the late 80's, and suffered blindly through the process. When I finally read about the emotional upheaval one goes through, similar to the "dark night of the soul" Christian mystics experience, I felt confirmed that I had indeed had "chakra awakenings."

4. Sjoo, Monica, and Barbara Mor in their book, *The Great Cosmic Mother*, report about the "inductor theory," as Mary Jane Sherfey's,(M.D.) discovery is called. In 1961, Dr. Sherfey found that "All mammalian embryos, male and

female, are anatomically female during the early stages of fetal life." Apparently it had been proven back in 1951, but kept secret by the male dominated medical profession. P. 3.

5. Monica Sjoo & Barbara Mor, *The Great Cosmic Mother*,p. 4.

6. I believe Mitra claimed that my second chakra was "awake" because I liked to have fun and was emotionally reactive. I had not yet begun healing my wounded child. My having "fun" was more out of escape than natural enjoyment of life.

Mitra, as do most teachers of Eastern philosophy and spirituality, taught that the first three chakras were in a sense negative and to be "risen above," or in some other way controlled.

I instinctively disagreed with this teaching. As I continued to listen to my instincts I discovered that the second chakra was indeed the "womb" chakra. "Why would teachers, both in Western religion and Eastern religions teach the degradation of this chakra? Indeed, the first three chakras?"

7. For more in-depth information about the Five Elements I recommend Dianne Connelly's book, *Traditional Acupuncture: The Law Of The Five Elements*. The description of Earth Element begins on page 65.

8. By the time I did the exercises to awaken this chakra I had been doing Buddhist chanting in conjunction with my shiatsu training (although Ohashi would say I made a very poor "sitter"), and crying and yelling a lot—my wounded child was uncontrollably surfacing due to all the hara and emotional work from the awakening of the first two chakras.

When doing exercises to awaken this center, it literally felt like a cord was pulling out my navel. It was a gut wrenching experience. This happened about three times. One I remember in particular after I had done a sweat lodge. When I got out of the sweat the gut wrenching cord started to pull on my navel. Soon I was doubled over on the ground seeing a huge tiger eye. I went into the iris of the eye and became a milky white crystal formation. I *became* the crystal.

This kind of experience is common when we are awakening the "Inner Senses". Afterward, I craved steak n' eggs! Interestingly enough, beef is the food associated with Earth Element in the Law of the Five Elements.

9. Bentov, Itzhak, *Stalking The Wild Pendulum*, P. 175.

10. Stone, Merlin, *When God Was A Woman*, was published in 1976. I feel there is a connection between the interest in the Goddess religions and the reawakening of an interest in Shamanism that was popularized by Michael Harner's classic, *The Way of the Shaman*, published in 1980.

2

The Cycle
Of The
Emotions

I AM SummerWomb, AutumnWomb, WinterWomb, SpringWomb. I am GriefCompassion, FearCompassion, AngerCompassion. I am the BabyMother, ChildMother, AdolescentMother, AdultMother of your time on Mother Earth.

I am SunWonderChild, ColoredLeaves WonderChild, SnowWhiteWonderChild, and GreenBabyLeafWonderChild. I spiral and intertwine each of these into the fabric of your being and you feel me through the Cycles of your emotions.

ALL of the emotions are LOVE. Fear is frozen LOVE. Compassion is balanced LOVE. Anger is unidentified, or unrecognized, or unowned LOVE. Sadness is a sense of lost LOVE. Grief is the loss of a loved one or loss of an opportunity for LOVE. LOVE is ALL there is.

Affirmation:
LOVE is All-That-Is. I am LOVE
when I fear. I am LOVE when I'm
angry. I am LOVE when I am sad.
I am LOVE when I grieve the loss of
LOVE. I am LOVE when I am
happy. I am innately good and my
natural state of being comes from
LOVE.

The Cycle of the Emotions

When you allow your emotions
their natural spontaneous flow they will never
engulf you, and always return you refreshed to "logical"
conscious-mind thought. It is only when you dam them up
that they appear to be opposed to the intellect,
or overwhelming.

— Seth
The Nature of Personal Reality
Session 646, March 7, 1973

P eople fight feeling their feelings and have been taught to do so for centuries resulting in their denying and projecting their emotions in many subtle ways of which they are not aware. They armor their bodies and their lives from their feelings, for fear they will be engulfed by them.

In making sure we humans do not feel anger, grief, sadness, and fear, we unknowingly create barriers between ourselves and others. The more disconnected we become from these feelings, the more shallowly we breathe. The more shallowly we breathe the more we cut off oxygen to our organs, in particular, the liver, gall bladder, kidneys, bladder and intestines, i.e., the lower part of our bodies, and the first three chakras.

These first three chakras is where the childself resides. Especially the wounded childself lives here. S/he is our emotional source. S/he is the accumulation of all we have felt emotionally in all of our life times, especially this one. We become so invested in not feeling the scared and hurt child within that our bladders and kidneys have urinary infections, kidney stones, and need dialysis machines to keep our "frozen in fear" bodies functioning. As long as we deny our hurts and pains, cover them up with drugs, or blame our circumstances on someone or something outside of us we think we are safe from feeling some uncontrollable demon deep down inside of us. Or, perhaps, we do lose control on a regular basis and holler or cry often never seeming to go beyond being angry and/or depressed. We have opened the door to the emotions, stepped into either a persecutor or victim role and don't dare go any further. Or, we don't want to go any further. Yelling (persecutor role) and crying (victim role) bring us what we want in life. Or, so it seems.

I call this ingrained denial and projection of feeling "kicking and screaming". It paradoxically describes the silent kicking and screaming of the emotions that are going on inside a person when he or she is doing all s/he can to not feel. Excuses and physical armoring are the main forms of kicking and screaming. Another popular form of "kicking and screaming" is to deny feelings and blame others way beyond the incident. These patterns are well established by age ten.

By adult age we are working pretty hard to maintain them and when our hold on denying feelings or projecting onto others is in any way threatened, intellectual kicking and screaming flares up to protect them.

To a sensitive person it feels like kicking and screaming. In my case, I feel my body cringe and my ears shut off to an internal noise these unowned feelings make. I feel as if I am being abused. To a sensitive person denial of feelings is abuse. If someone else is denying the feelings, it feels like external abuse. If the sensitive person is denying his or her own feelings, s/he usually feels intense pain somewhere in the body. If someone is projecting onto me, I also feel pain somewhere, usually in my neck. This ability used to be a "real pain in the neck" and now it's a gift especially working with clients and in giving workshops.

The closer we get to entering the cycle of the emotions, the more obvious is the kicking and screaming. The more threatened we feel the more we do what has worked in the past even if not appropriate anymore. Many clients in any form of psychotherapy, who are about to begin feeling their feelings, often drop out of therapy. The fear feels too great to go on. Many others get stuck in one or more of the emotions, such as a person who is often yelling and blaming is stuck in anger which is usually a cover up for fear. For those people it's as though they are stuck in the negative aspect of one or more of the seasons.

For instance, being stuck in anger is like being stuck year round in the howling winds of spring. Being stuck in fear is like being frozen year round in the ice of winter. Being stuck in grief is like being stuck for a year in a gloomy fall day watching dead brown leaves fall to the ground. Being stuck in sympathy is like being stuck in constant change and having no life of your own. Being stuck in sadness is like having it rain every day for the whole summer.

The *cycles of the seasons* show us the cycles of the emotions. They move one into the other monthly, year after year. Even in a frigid or tropical climate there are seasons and movement from one to another. When emotions are experienced as the changing of the seasons: summer love moves into the "wisdom to trust" of fall moves into the "courage to change" of winter moves into the "power to be" winds of spring and moves into a summer of love once again. Cushioned between each season is compassion, a compassion for self and others and a compassion for All-That-Is.

This cycle is the natural and healthy one. It is natural and healthy to feel and to flow with the tides and waves of emotions. To dam them up is to drown our beingness in stagnant water and to cause drought and famine downstream in our relationship with ourselves and others and on our planet.

A person carrying around a wounded child inside of him or her is being run by the degree of pain oozing daily from the wound. If the initial wound occurred at age three and it didn't get healed then the adult self is being run, emotionally, by a three year old.

Imagine a top executive of an oil company, at age four, witness his father beat up his mother. The child freezes in fear and eventually learns to numb himself emotionally. After he sees this scene often enough he learns to disrespect women. He further learns to shut down anything equated with being feminine such as feelings, compassion for other species and being vulnerable in any way. A pattern of denial of emotions and projection of feelings and responsibility for them becomes a way of life. It is a socially accepted way of life in his culture. In fact he is praised for his shrewd business mind, football player strategy and his unemotional ability to "get the job done".

An oil spill occurs (a massive symbol, perhaps, of the blood oozing from his child self wounds) and gallons of crude oil from this executive's company ship washes up on a shore line maiming countless fowl, fish, turtles and other sea animals. Miles of beach are destroyed. He hardly notices. He sees only the dollar bill loss of the oil, the company time lost, and the repair bill of the oil tanker. He is not necessarily selfish and greedy. He simply can't emotionally afford to feel the damage done to nature and the wildlife. If he does, a very hurt and scared four year old, inside of him, might blubber out the many, many years of accumulated emotional pain.

The repressing of his emotions is done automatically and unconsciously. He has repressed and denied them for so long that he might not even remember that his father was abusive toward his mother. When asked how far back he remembers into his childhood he might say, "Five or six..."

When the childhood decisions made in reaction to traumas arrest a person emotionally, the natural flow of the emotions become dammed. Years later this dammed up stream becomes ten or more times its original size. The muscles where the memories are stored harden and tighten forming a coat of armor. This armoring is the stream of emotions frozen and swollen into the muscle fibers. These armored muscles hold an electrical charge detectable by sensitive others and the sentics machine.[1]

The cellular memory banks in the persons' body record and electrically hold the emotional memories until such time as they are discharged either by acupressure, hypnosis, some other form of healthy release, or pacified with an addiction, or, worst of all some one else feels it for the person. Acupressure, in particular Jin Shin Do and Shin Shiatsu, are effective methods of accessing the recorded childhood traumas. If an emotional trauma has been healed or is healing, it is hardly detectable via the pressure points, but if the person doesn't consciously remember or if the person is denying the emotions, they consolidate in the womb area and have a built up electrical charge that can be detected either emotionally or visually by trained sensitives.[2]

For example, if I quickly get a vision of the child self and an age as I cup my hands on the navel during a Shin Shiatsu session, then I know there is a wounded child within crying to be healed and free. I also fairly accurately guess that the person is afraid of feeling his or her feelings and is in denial of them. Of course there are body language signs. If s/he is not afraid to feel the emotions or is actively healing the wounded child self the vision does not jump out at me quite so quickly. I might not even detect the emotional pain of the wounded child self. Instead I will feel the energy of the healing process in progress.

It is the unowned emotional pain that people *in denial* release into their outer auric layers that sensitives (trained and untrained) pick up on. Virginia Satir, famous psychotherapist and trained sensitive shared her experiences of detecting people's emotional states via their auras:

"This is important to share with you because as I sit with a

32

family, my body tells me a great deal about where those people are and where their boundaries are. For example, the boundary is very, very close around a super-reasonable person. This is probably one of the reasons people say that the super-reasonable person is not 'available'. The boundary around an irrelevant person is all broken; you can't tell where it is. The boundary around a blamer is very far out and jagged. The placater is a very interesting person. His boundary is made out of liquid—out of whipped cream that is beginning to melt. It is there, but you can't tell much from it. Even though this is a somewhat picturesque way of talking about a person and his presence, it is something of which I am very aware, and I honor it. Perhaps a poetic way of putting it is this: What you are feeling at any point in time is how much of a person's life is willing to make itself known, with what fear, with what protectiveness. If you want to connect with that, you must be able to respect it.[3]

For untrained sensitives, feeling other people's feelings can be very disturbing. For instance, in feeling the jagged energy of a blamer, an untrained sensitive usually will take the feeling being projected as being her or his own. She or he will usually internalize these feelings and very likely become depressed. This can lead to many mental disorders. I am convinced that many of our sisters and brothers in depressed and other unhappy states of mind are not there just because of their own emotional baggage. They are probably carrying much of the rest of the family's unowned feelings as well.

Being a trained sensitive is an invaluable tool when assisting others to process and heal. And, yes, respect is important because a trained sensitive usually feels, especially, the unowned feelings of the client. Fear is usually the biggest item keeping clients from owning their feelings, so caution is necessary to bring them to the point of acknowledging emotions they have probably invested years in covering up and hiding from themselves. All of this has usually been unconsciously done. Presenting unowned feelings to people before they are ready often makes them react negatively and defensively. This is sometimes fine when the therapist knows that a client will stick it out and work through the issue. Sometimes it's tricky going when a sensitive knows more about what a person is feeling than the person does! In Shin Shiatsu I usually use the following steps:

1) I gently attempt to get the client to acknowledge the pain of a feeling. If s/he does not, that signals me to stop.[4] If the client *does* acknowledge the pain then the next step is to,

2) Ask permission to do an exercise to ascertain the possible originating experience(s). At the originating experience(s) is where life long decisions are made.

3) A healing process is chosen by the inner child and adult of the client.

The healing process is sometimes the hardest part because it often means changing self destructive behavior to a more positive and pleasurable way of living. Many people believe pleasure is "bad". Beliefs of this nature have to be changed before healing the wounded child can be effective and lasting.

Just as a parent might handle a kicking and screaming child with caution, and hopefully with compassion, if the reason is because the child is afraid of something, so is it important to handle clients gently who are in denial because of fear. For fearful clients, a courageous step has already been taken by being there for hands-on therapy. It's up to the sensitive/therapist to establish an atmosphere of reassurance, respect, and trust in order to continue on. This is especially true of hands-on sensitives working with people who were abused prior to age five. Touching allows the most armored of people an opportunity to feel safe enough to begin to get in touch with wounds that have been carried around for generations. But, many people do not move past the first two steps: (1) denial, (2) projection/transference, that make up the "kicking and screaming" phase. If that is a conscious choice, then I respect and honor that choice and recommend continuing with a "talk" form of psychotherapy.

Chapter Two Notes

1. The sentics machine was invented by Manford Clines, a musician. More information may be found in George Leonard's book, *The Silent Pulse*, p. 54.

2. A "trained sensitive" is an empath who may be in any of the healing professions.

3. Satir, Virginia, *Conjoint Family Therapy*, p.259.

4. I learned this lesson the hard way. I apologize to all the very wounded infants who were my clients, that I did not know this at the time I worked with you. I proceeded to use "push button" techniques, which scare wounded infants, and are in fact damaging. I forgive myself because I used the experience to reach out and learn. (I believe we can only forgive ourselves: We can heal our emotional reactions to what others do to us, but only they can forgive themselves for what they do.) I am now very compassionate when working with clients who have wounded infants inside.

3

In Knowing
How To
Die...

I am deathrebirth. In the brilliance of Autumn, each year, I show you the glory of rebirth into the ehteric dimension. And when you no longer fear me you will not be so obsessed and possessed to know me or to fight me or to worry about what I am like. Then, you will be able to Be yourself and get on with truly living.

Affirmation:
Each falling leaf that passes by my window is a lifetime of brilliance, joy, and greatness and I know I am the same.

There is no death. There is only transformation.

In Knowing How To Die...

Life is a state of becoming
and death is a part of this process of becoming.
You are alive now, a consciousness knowing itself, sparkling
with cognition amid a debris of dead and dying cells; alive
while the atoms and molecules of your body die and are reborn.
You are alive, therefore, in the midst of the death of yourself –
alive despite, and yet because of, the multitudinous deaths
and rebirths that occur within your body
in physical terms.

– Seth
Seth Speaks: The Eternal Validity Of The Soul.
Session 535, June 17, 1970

She was exhaling as forcefully as she was inhaling. Was she gasping for breath, trying to live? No, I thought, she's breathing too rhythmically. Each exhalation resembled a birthing contraction. For one and one-half hours she rhythmically rasped in eight counts, then out eight counts. Then she died.

I knew she wasn't dead. No one breathes like that for one and one-half hours without a birth also taking place. It was obvious to me, she was taking in air on each inhale to help herself leave her body on each exhale. It seemed like it took her the one and one-half hours to get up enough momentum to get her whole soul out on her last exhale.

Mom was 72 years old when she died. Her last gift to me was to convince me that death was birth. This gift of "knowing" freed me to see that when we go through life fearing death, we never really live. All our energy gets focused into preventing the many and constant "small deaths" inherent in living. Working hard to prevent something results in living in a kind of purgatory or limbo. Indecision, not knowing what one wants and not following one's bliss are all signs of "fear of dying" in some intangible way.

Continuously staying in purgatory or limbo eventually destroys zest and reason for living. Containing and controlling the emotions, in this way, effects the biochemistry so that tension forming biochemicals flood the internal organs causing all kinds of havoc. Dammed up anger attacks the gall bladder. Stuck in expressing anger attacks the liver and eventually the heart. A vessel full of fear overloads the kidneys, adrenals and the bladder. Held back grief slows down the energy flow into the lungs and large intestine. Repressed emotions, in general, get stuck in the lungs and large intestine, which are the two main eliminators of physical wastes as well as being emotional avenues for expression and release.

Remorse and sadness bleed the heart and small intestine as in bleeding ulcers. Constant denial of the wounded child within beats on the reproductive system and the organs that nurture it which are the stomach and pancreas. The more wounded the child, the more effort goes into thinking instead of feeling. Stomach and spleen (pancreas) meridians either get over loaded or depleted with energy when this happens.

Heart and small intestine energy are fed by the stomach and pancreas (spleen meridian) energy which flow into the kidney and bladder energy. An over fed wounded child eventually puts too much of a load on the heart. A feared and, therefore, denied wounded child, exacts so much energy from the kidney and bladder energies that the heart gets depleted and doesn't have enough energy to keep its rhythm or to cleanse itself. High cholesterol and arrhythmia are often signs of a denied wounded child. It is no coincidence that heart disease is the number one killer in America today.

If we aren't emotionally living, then we are dying. One way to prevent the dying process from constantly killing life is, ironically, to die. Not physically, although our cells do that naturally, but by dying into the emotion at hand. If you are angry, be angry. If you are sad, be sad, etc. Physical symptoms connected with each emotion also need to be allowed expression. For instance, a person who has been fearful for most of her life may find herself having to urinate frequently for a period of time as she chooses to be more courageous and make changes in her life. The emotions and the physical dis-eases that accompany them are cleansing tools, not hostile aliens invading our souls. When we fight them we are only fighting ourselves. An underlying belief that we are not naturally good is usually in operation. Being emotional and having dis-eases are nature's way of raining out of our body-mind what we no longer need. It is only when we fight the emotions and the dis-eases that we distort them and make them into something they never intended to be, such as cancer.

There is one other important belief that contributes to us fighting ourselves. It is a belief that there is no life after physical death. Consequently, we spend inordinate amounts of energy and money making sure we do not physically die. We take all kinds of cold suppressants, cough suppressants and pain suppressants so we won't know those symptoms are there. Why? Because we believe, ultimately, if they get out of hand we will die.

Most of the rules in the work place are based on that belief. Yet, only if colds, aches and pains do get out-of-hand, are people rewarded with sick leave and sympathy.

A balanced, compassionate way of doing this would be to trust the inner knowing of a worker that s/he is coming down with a cold, which is nature's way of saying the body needs a rest and the person cheerfully given a day or two off to rest, relax, and even have a good time, if that's what is needed.

The belief that there is no life after physical death is subtle. We constantly feed it by participating in a health care and insurance system that financially rewards only the sick. We feed it by supporting a religion that keeps us fearful of a devil that'll get us "if we don't watch out". We believe in our human worthlessness when we believe a boss or institution, outside ourselves, knows what's better for us than we do. We gladly sell our souls and responsibility for them, to an "out there" that will somehow keep us physically immortal and therefore, we believe, safe from being possessed by a demon or dying.

Underneath it all, we want to believe there is life after death. We naturally yearn to live forever because some aspect deep inside of us *knows* that we do. It is a natural, built in reminder from God/Goddess/All-That-Is that our essence never dies. It is the belief and fear that there is no joyful heaven after death we all go to, that keeps us stuck in fear and, ironically constantly dying.

Core NDErs (near death experiencers) bring us back one great gift! The vast majority no longer fear death. In no longer fearing death, they begin to live self-actualized lives:

From the study of the NDE, we have learned to see death in a new way, not as something to be dreaded but, on the contrary, as an encounter with the Beloved. Those who can come to understand death in this way, as NDErs, are compelled to, need never fear death again. And liberated from this primary fear, they too, like NDErs, become free to experience life as the gift it is and to live naturally, as a child does, with delight. Not everyone can have or needs to have an NDE, but everyone can learn to assimilate these lessons of the NDE into his own life if he chooses to.[2]

The key to living and letting go of fear is the word "choose". The fearful person says, "I can't, I can't..." The courageous person acknowledges the fear, then chooses whether to, or not to take the next step. It's as though a person must be willing to die in order to live. A person willing to die says, "I'm scared and I'll do it anyway." Then s/he educates her or himself as to what best suits her or his way of doing things to move through, or out of, whatever unwanted situation s/he is in.

The fear of death, or annihilation (one workshop participant said this word scared her more) faces us daily. Each time we play the role of victim we are choosing "fear of death" to be our god of the moment.

NDErs and self-actualized people, who also no longer fear death, go through a period of adjustment that can best be described as emotional house cleaning. It may also mean changing jobs, locations and/or relationships. It upsets others at first, who are co-dependant upon the old roles the becoming self-actualized people played. The act of staying focused in being true to oneself, is a very loving one in the long run. What more loving gift can one ask for than a person be truly who s/he is and to love you, in turn, truly as you are?

When Mom died, I grieved for the woman I never got to know. Mom always did what would look good to the outside world. She sacrificed her true self to "should's" and "I can'ts" because "What would they think?" and eventually ate herself up with it in the form of liver and pancreatic cancer. At the time she died, the song, "The Rose",was popular. The line, "and it's the soul afraid of dying that never learns to live," fully expressed my grief for Mom. I decided I would learn to live as my return gift to her.

In the *AWAKENING THE WONDER CHILD PLAYSHOP*, one of the most effective exercises is the death and rebirth ceremony. When we consciously play act through our biggest fear to the point of rebirth then, to some degree, we release our fear of death. This has to be done as a cellular-level-energy experience. In other words, it has to be experienced at a gut level, in particular, the root and womb energy centers. People who have lost loved ones very close to them and have visited spirit world, core near death experiencers, adult children severely abused as children, and adults who didn't forget their extraordinary abilities and know that there is no death, that there is only transformation and know this at the core of their being, no longer fear death. People who haven't had these experiences, or have totally forgotten, have a hard time believing any of it is possible.

The knowledge that there is life after death has to be *experienced* by our very cells, or we don't get this innate knowledge reawakened. Long ago, as a species, when we disconnected from our biospirituality, we disconnected from this innate knowledge. Because it is natural and a part of our being, it stored itself in our cellular memory banks waiting to be reawakened to consciousness.[3] It is only logical that we have to get our consciousness to that cellular level in order to remember. Everyone who reaches that level comes up with the same conclusion: There is life after death.[4]

The next most important outcome is that when this knowledge has been integrated these people really begin enjoying this life. Please note that many years may be spent between the reawakening and the enjoying, cleaning up the mess in-between, i.e., contrived beliefs, child-self wounds, and all of the patterns created from years of investment in the consequences of those energy distortions before the "enjoying" can fully be actualized.

According to P.M.H. Atwater's research, it takes seven years for a near-death survivor to begin to reintegrate into this life. Biologically it takes seven years for every cell in the body to die and be reborn. Any cellularly experienced trip to spirit world, not just those of near death experiencers, results in this life transforming journey. According to P.M.H. Atwater,

> *The near death experience, if successfully integrated, seems to put the individual in phase with nature and on track with the natural ebb and flow of life's energies. We feel better, are more at ease and invigorated; our place in the scheme of things seems more assured, and life itself is more understandable.*[5]

She further states:

It is the quality of life, not the number of years lived, that determines the worth of life. Those who have shifted consciousness know this.[6]

I first read about the idea of quality of life in Jane Roberts', *The Individual And The Nature Of Mass Events* about ten years ago. I immediately recognized it as true. It jumped out at me verifying a hope and longing I'd carried since my childhood when I spent many hours out on our family farm and on the mountain behind our house. I hoped that someday our own species would learn this. The concept still serves as a beacon of light for me about the meaning of physical life:

Survival of course, is important, but it is not the prime purpose of a species, in that it is a necessary means by which that species can attain its goals. Of course a species must survive to do so, but it will, however, purposefully avoid survival if the conditions are not practically favorable to maintain the quality of life or existence that is considered basic.[7]

On our farm in Michigan the animals are continuously teaching me about biological spirituality. Several times I have had the privilege of assisting our veterinary with the act of euthanasia when one of the goats is too old to continue having a "quality" of life. It is our policy to telepathically communicate with a goat and to ask her if euthanasia is what she wants.

She signifies by allowing me to gently turn her head sideways so that the veterinary can insert the needle into a blood vessel in her neck. There is no struggle. I do not use any force. A flock of geese or cranes usually fly over the day the transformation is to take place. For me this is another sign that spirit world is preparing for the transformation.

Animals in the wild orchestrate their own kind of euthanasia:

In many animal groups the sick animal isolates itself for a period of rest, in which it is also free to seek out those natural conditions most conducive to its health. It travels to find certain herbs, or it lies in the mud or clay by certain rivers...

When and if it is killed by its brothers, this is not an act of cruelty but an innate understanding that the creature can no longer operate physically without agony; a quite natural euthanasia is involved, in which the 'patient' also acquiesces.[8]

This acquiescence to euthanasia by our goats, and how my mother died proved to me that death is rebirth. In knowing that our individual spirit does not die we are freed to more fully live!

Chapter Three Notes

1. A "core" near death experiencer is one who consciously remembers his or her experience into an after world. Those who vividly remember, usually have a more positive outlook on it and are better able to relax into enjoying the rest of this physical life. Many, who have near death experiences do not remember them. Their beliefs and ways of living do not change as remarkably as those who remember.

2. Ring, Kenneth, *Heading Toward Omega*, P. 268.

3. According to Seth our cellular memory banks carry information from the past and future as well as the present. Our physical cells also remember every physical form they have ever been a part of, and therefore, carry our innate ability to empathize with All That Is.

4. Please note: Not everyone who has had NDE, for instance, remembers to this level. One's beliefs play a major role in what is and isn't remembered.

5. Atwater, P.M.H., *Coming Back To Life, The After Effects Of The Near Death Experience*, p.190.

6. Ibid. p. 193.

7. Roberts, Jane. *The Individual and the Nature of Mass Events*, Session 805, May 16, 1977.

8. Ibid. Session 661, May 7, 1973, 11:55PM

4

A Passion

for

Living

I am the simple pleasures that feed your passion and zest for a bioSpiritual life. I can be found in your daily joys—a greatly enjoyed cup of coffee or tea, a transcending moment of watching a sunrise or sunset, hypnotic lapping of water upon the shore, the consciousness altering trickle of a small brook, the joy of your children, the playfulness of kittens and puppies, the special touch of your grandmother, and the smell of Mom's freshly baked pie...

I am passion for living and you enjoy me most when you give yourself permission to truly desire and receive my pleasures. In turn you give far more joy to others when you are following your own bliss. The more you enjoy yourself, the more love you have to give to others and All-That-Is.

Affirmation: I am consciousness and bliss absolute. I am sat-chit-ananada. The more pleasure and creativity I have in my life, the more love and compassion I can give to others.

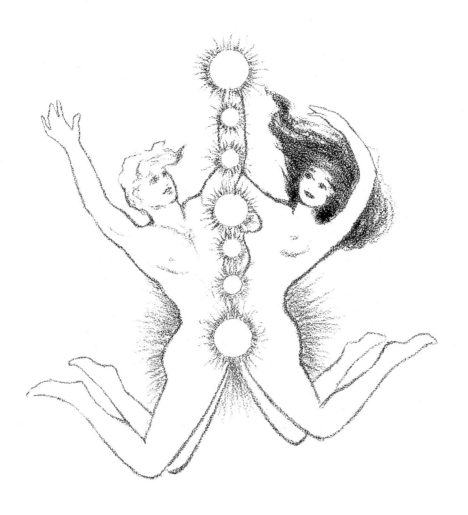

...they protect their time, say "no" to unrewarding social invitations, recoil naturally and without much guilt-from toxic people, situations, jobs, and responsibilities...and describe their efforts as a way to demonstrate their affection for others and to grow in respect for themselves.[1]

It stands to reason if we aren't doing what we love, i.e., practicing pleasure, then we aren't loving ourselves and certainly can't honestly love others. Practicing pleasure develops our self-worth. Jane Roberts, in speaking as Seth says:

Love, as it is often experienced, allows an individual to take his sense of self-worth from another for a time and to at least momentarily let the other's beliefs in his goodness supersede his own belief in lack of worth. Again, I make a distinction between this and a greater love in which two individuals, knowing their own worth, are able to give and receive.[2]

It is the greater love that comes from practicing passion and joy in being, and developing self-esteem that enables a person to love unconditionally. Even in times of pain, sadness, grief, fear, and anger there is an underlying compassion and knowing that the brief moment of physical or emotional pain is a "good hurt" that is precipitating a life-giving change.

"It hurts so good," is a commonly made statement by my and other body-mind worker's clients. They know the "hurt-good" (not suffering) heals. They feel it healing. This feel good hurt is a loving way to move the emotional pain behind it sometimes transforming months, years, and lifetimes of hurt into a pleasurable release and letting go.

Repeatedly healing body-mind hurts can transform a life attitude from one of pain seeking, to pleasure seeking, and from pleasure seeking to pleasure giving. Sharing pleasure/love is what two self-actualized people do.

When the wounded child is healed enough and a person feels more and more worthwhile, loved, and loving, then the seemingly mundane takes on a sensation of being pleasurable. Watching an ant, for instance, can become an exhilarating experience.

Practicing this kind of pleasure strengthens biospirituality until pleasure becomes a daily spiritual act. Spiritual pleasure is about being able to feel, process, grow and keep on enjoying living. It's about feeling capable and empowered to handle feelings and all the body-mind expressions of them without selling out your needs and wants. It's about owning the personal power to Be. It's about being able to move through, and not get stuck in, depression, disease, and powerlessness. It's about being able to live happily and harmoniously with the one person you'll never be without: You!

As a result, a personal distinction between spiritual practice and addictive behavior can be developed . (See next page)

I suggest you make your own chart of pleasurable spiritual practices and addictions. Then, own the power to choose which you will practice at any given time. Sometimes choosing to practice an addiction gives us a needed insight or a moment of escape that is not only wanted but needed. The key to staying empowered is in the "choosing". In consciously "choosing" and "not choosing" to participate in an addiction we are, in fact, moving into using certain practices as pleasures.

Feeling powerless to choose means more emotional house cleaning is in order. Hopping from addiction to addiction to addiction also means the emotional homework is not done. I've seen many alcohol abusers go from alcohol to coffee, to cigarettes, to food, to meditation, to religion, to work, etc., without addressing the underlying issues of the wounded child within. Addictions are a cry from within that our child self has needs and wants that s/he wants and needs taken of.

How old is the emotional child that runs your life? That is usually a substantial clue as to what age your child-self was emotionally wounded.

Biospiritual Practice		Addiction	
BIOSPIRITUAL PRACTICE	THE RESULTING PLEASURE	ACTING OUT BEHAVIOR	THE RESULTING PAIN
Sex as expression of intimacy and love.	A first, second and fourth chakra orgasm. And/or a feeling of at-One-ment. A renewed passion for living.	Sex as a tension release or act of power, such as in sexual addictions, incest, rape and "power over" sex.	Often due to experiencing abuse and male/female imbalance in the opposite sex parent.
Giving a gift because you want to.	The pleasure of having someone receive your love in material and/or thought form	Giving a gift because you feel you should or because you'll feel guilty if you don't.	Fear of abandonment if you don't please others. Low self-esteem.
Acknowledging being angry about something and expressing it to the point of transformation.	Expressing anger to transformation, but not at someone, opens the door to intimacy, honesty and frees LOVE.	Denying being angry or afraid. Repressing expressing anger to the point of healing it. Or, covering up fear with anger, i.e. often acting angry with no resolution.	Fear of evil, which shows itself as a belief that anger is bad or wrong.
Eating only what the body needs at the first chakra level, i.e. "physical need" level.	A sensation of "making love" to your food. The food energies feel appreciated, and you get more nutrients out of what you need.	Eating without tasting or feeling the essence of the food. Eating to satisfy longing for nurturing.	The child in you is not feeling loved.
Physical movement that feels good physically emotionally, and spiritually.	A sense of union of spirit with flesh, i.e. biospirituality.	Participating in a sport or physical activity to relieve tension of getting high on activity without addressing the reason for the need to get high.	feeling "not good enough." Compensates by looking outside-of-self for validation.

If you do not have a sense of your emotional age and do not sense a wonder child inside, then you can be pretty sure that you were emotionally abused as a child. (Assuming that you have chosen to be mentally and intellectually capable this life-time.)

Yet, it is the Wonder child in you that urges you on to seek out ways to heal the wounded child and to have genuine pleasure in life. A sense of child-like wonder is biologically encoded and is the "joy" energy in our bio-spirituality. It is a natural bio-spiritual right to enjoy life.

This inner power is expressed through our impulses. Using definition "c" in the New World Dictionary, an impulse is "a motive or tendency coming from within (prompted by an impulse of curiosity)." Using the same dictionary and defining its distortion as compulsive: "an irresistible, repeated irrational impulse to perform some act", I will state that spontaneous child-like wonder shows itself through impulses to act. Even thinking something through still results in a wholesome choice being made through our impulses. If we do not include our impulses – "tendency coming from within" – in a decision then we dam up that natural flow of energy and most often carry the stress in our shoulders, necks, and upper backs. Seth states that,

When you are taught not to trust your impulses you begin to lose your powers of decision, and to whatever extent involved in the circumstances, you begin to lose your sense of power because you are afraid to act.[4]

Seth further states that impulses are altruistic:

Psychologically, your impulses are as vital to your being as your physical organs are. They are as altruistic, or unselfish, as your physical organs...impulses are doorways to action, satisfaction, the exertion of natural mental and physical power, the avenue for your private expression—the avenue where your private expression intersects the physical world and impresses it.[5]

The more we trust our natural impulses the more spontaneous we are and the more often we are acting out of a sense of child-like wonder and awe and curiosity that *benefits* us and All-That-Is. What fun to be loving and feel loved all at the same time!

One of our most untapped and unexplored sources of inner impulse power can be found in the gifts of our emotions.

Chapter Four Notes

1. Sinetar, Marsha, *Ordinary People As Monks And Mystics*, p.148.

2. Roberts, Jane. *The Nature Of Personal Reality*, session 661,May 7, 1973.

3. Definitions taken from *Webster's New World Dictionary*, second college edition, Simon and Schuster, 1986.

4. Roberts, Jane, *The Individual And The Nature Of Mass Events*, session 860, June 13, 1979.

5. Roberts, Jane, *The Individual And The Nature Of Mass Events*, session 857, May 30, 1979.

Imagination
and emotions are
the most concentrated forms
of energy that you possess as
physical creatures. Any strong
emotion carries within it far
more energy than, say, that
required to send a rocket to the moon.
Emotions, instead of propelling a physical
rocket, for example, send thoughts
from this interior reality through
the barrier between nonphysical and
physical into the "objective" world—
no small feat, and one that is
constantly repeated.

— Seth
The Nature Of Personal Reality,
Session 625, November, 1972

55

5

The Power
Of The
Emotions

I am the power that activates or subdues your passion for living. I am the action aspect of your emotions. I am regulated by your beliefs and your decisions about your experiences. I am consciously active whether you choose to be aware of me or not. I influence your every thought and so-called logical process. I color your world in the color of me that you concentrate upon.

I am the daily weather in your mind. I am your feeling tone of the moment. If you trust me I am a safe ship for you to ride through the depths of your feelings to the mountain peaks of your emotions.

Affirmation:
I trust the power of my emotions. I know they are here to cleanse me like a gentle rain; to shake me awake like a thunderstorm; to bring me the sunshine of my life. I trust my emotions. I trust me.

CHAPTER FIVE

The Power Of The Emotions

*Dogmas or systems of thought
that tell you to rise above your emotions can be
misleading-even, in your terms, dangerous. Such theories
are based upon the concept that there is something innately
disruptive, base, or wrong in man's emotional nature, while
the soul is always depicted as being calm, "perfect," passive
and unfeeling. Only the most lofty, blissful awareness is
allowed. Yet, the soul is above all a fountain of energy,
creativity, and action that shows its characteristics in life
precisely through the ever changing emotions.*

SETH
The Nature Of Personal Reality,
Session 673, June 27, 1973.

I see a baby loving you from the spirit world," I said with my hands are cupped around Inez's navel.

"That's my daughter, Jean Ann." Inez rolls over to her side and curls up in the fetal position.

"Did she die young?" I ask and at the same time I'm seeing trauma and darkness with no form.

"I aborted her when I was three months..." Inez begins to cry.

"She's come to give you a message." I tell Inez, as the aspect of Jean Ann comes stronger into my clairsentience. I ask Inez if she feels guilty for having the abortion.

"Yes and mostly no. I knew it was the best for both of us, I just wasn't sure if Jean Ann agreed..." Inez cries harder.

"Can you feel Jean Ann's presence?" I calmly ask Inez.

"Yes, I feel her," Inez replies through her tears.

"What is she saying to you?" I ask, sensing Jean Ann attempting to communicate to Inez.

Through tears that are beginning to relax into sniffles, Inez replies, "She says she didn't come to be born, she came just to say 'hi' and to have me feel her love."

I ask Inez to wrap her arms around herself and to feel Jean Ann in her arms hugging her. "Do you feel her love?" I ask at the point I see her experiencing Jean Ann in her arms.

"Yes...very much," Inez is half whispering and mostly hugging and loving herself through the nonphysical presence of Jean Ann's essence.

As Inez allowed her nonphysical baby to hug her and love her, she relaxed and became the baby being loved.

"Who's hugging you now?" I ask her.

"My mother," she whispered.

"How old are you?"

"I'm two months." Inez looks and feels calm and peaceful.

"Was that a comforting time for you?" I ask.

"Yes," she answers.

"Then suck your thumb and pretend it's your mother nursing you," I gently urge as I place my right hand on her sacrum and feel very warm energy pass through it to Inez's womb. At the same time I place the middle finger of my left hand on a pressure point between her third and fourth thoracic vertebra. It is a major point effecting the lungs. Combined with the sacral pressure points, it feeds energy for self-love and self-worth.

Inez had been in therapy for several months after the abortion. This helped greatly to make Inez ready to accept the love from her baby, the nurturing healing from her mother and most importantly, herself. She said she felt her abdomen relax and that she was confident what she had done was Jean Ann's choice as well.

There are many who would say communication with the deceased, especially an undeveloped fetus, is not possible. Then, there are many who would say it is. What I have seen to be true is that for those who believe it is not possible, it isn't and for those who believe it is, it is.

It is not whether this form of communication can be scientifically proven or not that matters. It is the resulting inner peace and satisfaction gained and the emotional wound healed, that attest to this worthwhile subjective experience.

From my work with hundreds of people both in workshops and private sessions, I observed that for communication with a deceased loved one to have a meaningful impact, the following has to occur:

1) At a heightened emotional state (sadness, grief and sometimes anger or fear) the client enters into a mutual plane with the deceased loved one where clairvoyantly seeing, clairaudiently hearing or clairsentiently feeling the deceased loved one can take place. As a facilitator, I am in a semipermeable parallel state of consciousness where I feel my electricity adjust to fit theirs while remaining very calm and non-judgmental.

2) When emotional business is complete with the deceased loved one there is a noticeable shift of energy in the client. If I clairsentiently feel the first, second and third energy centers strong and balanced, I know the emotional business is finished. In an emotionally heightened state, the client also knows whether s/he is finished or not.

3) When a major shift is done at a certain emotional pitch, to completion, a cellular memory change also takes place. This is exemplified by changes in body temperature,

feeling the relief of long term muscle pain or tension and a calming of the previously erratic electrical field around the person's body.

After a meaningful impact a person may experience "a letting go" via the bodily functions such as increased activity in defecation and urination. In women, a menstrual period might start after the session even though it isn't due for another week or more. Plugged ears may all of a sudden unplug. One person reported her vision got better. In terms of the meridians, there is a correlation between the emotion healed, the meridian it is connected with and the organ involved. For example, a person letting go of long term fear may find herself urinating triple the number of times she usually does for about three to seven days. The meridians involved with fear are bladder and kidney. The physiological changes indicate a cellular memory change.

The concept of "cellular memory" came to me through the teachings of Seth and his suggested experiment:

Try a simple experiment. The results will be self-explanatory. Think of a sad event from your life. Similar feelings will soon follow, and with them memories of other such unpleasant episodes strung together through association. Scenes, odors, words, perhaps half-forgotten, will suddenly come upon you with new freshness. Your thoughts will activate the appropriate feelings. Beneath your awareness, however, they will also trigger the cells' ever-present memory imprints of stimuli received when those events occurred. There is, to some extent now, a cellular memory playback—and on the part of the entire body, the recognition of its state at that time.

If you pursue such sorrowful thoughts persistently, you are reactivating that body condition. Think of one of the most pleasant events that ever happened to you and the reverse will be true, but the process is the same. This time the associated memories are pleasant, and the body changes accordingly.[1]

Using this concept I healed and continue to heal my own child-self wounds and have taught it to hundreds of others who have also found it works. From this concept I developed the healing of the inner child aspect of Shin Shiatsu. Again, it does not matter whether the client believes in spirit world communication, reincarnation or regression back to childhood. What matters is the emotional experience, and the beliefs about the experience. It is usually the emotions grief, anger, sadness, or fear, which all stem from a deep love, that are the vehicles into a sense of no time and space. A dark tunnel or void in the zone of no-sense-of-space-and-time is entered. In it, or at the end of it, voices, visions, odors, and sometimes physical symptoms of loved ones, either deceased or still physically alive, are experienced as real. In an emotional state a return to re-experiencing childhood memories is more possible and helps bring up repressed memories. The more that is remembered, the deeper the healing possible.

In the depths of the emotions one can change the past. By change I mean, alter its impact from one of hurt and pain to simply remembering with no adverse emotional reaction. Some clients have actually changed the memory and made it a pleasant one. Once a memory is cellularly changed, it does not come back to "haunt" you. The emotion is complete for that incident.

To change a cellular memory a self-introduced vision of another probable way things-could-have-been is inserted just after the pinnacle of emotional expression has been reached. Timing, ironically, is most important in this realm of no-time or space. I check with the person to see if s/he can see or feel the presence or hear the voice of the loved one just as the expression of fear, anger, grief, or sadness feels to me like it has passed it's peak of expression. Then I ask the person how s/he would have liked it to have been.

Without exception, the underlying desires are:

1) **To be loved** and/or

2) **To be recognized as worthwhile** by a certain loved one.

The expression of those desires vary from individual to individual. One person was deeply touched by having his imagined father tell him he loved him as an infant. He perceived that his "real" father never did. As I had him have his conjured father tell him that several times, I also had him lovingly caress his face and arms. As in NLP (Neurolinguistic Programming), the touching anchors the new and more desirable sensation of being loved. When done in an emotionally heightened state the re-programming lasts and actually changes the person's cellular memory of a past event. The re-programming usually has to be done for each traumatic event and eventually takes only a few minutes to do. The touching combined with the re-parenting works best for child-self wounds incurred in infancy through the pre-school age.

By school age, the verbal re-programming works best with maybe a quick hug. Touching isn't as necessary unless there are still unhealed infancy through school age wounds mixed together. This is quite common.

None of the re-parenting works unless a person is able to fully get into feeling his or her feelings. People who are in denial are not doing it on purpose. It is usually because of great fear. Their beliefs will reflect that fear in their willingness and ability to express anger. I use anger as the test emotion. A person stuck in fear cannot and will not express anger even if it's pretend.

Another favorite form of denial people are often stuck in is intellectualism. Virginia Satir defines these people as "super-reasonable". In a Shin Shiatsu session they control movement of their heads, legs, and arms by lifting them when I go to move them or by moving their heads, legs, and arms into the next position when they think that's what I'm going to do next. They keep their energy from going any farther down than the top part of the lungs. Their breathing is usually limited to their upper body as well. Deep relaxation is unknown to them even if they are very athletic.

An intellectually inserted belief about changing the pains of the past does not work. For instance, two conflicting beliefs, "I can't do anything about the past," felt at the childself level and "I can heal my past," affirmed only mentally, produce a war in the body with various dis-eases or accidents resulting. Most dis-eases effect the heart, blood and/or blood vessels. It is in the heart energy center where intellect and emotions meet and intermix. A person who says, "Yes, but...," and "But, what if...," is usually displaying coexisting conflicting beliefs.

Not until a change occurs in the second energy center simultaneously with a belief change can the true powers of the emotions be awakened. When there is physical vibration in the second energy center, such as crying, certain breathing techniques, and gut-level yelling can bring about, then there is a cellular memory opening and re-programming can take place. Accidents represent the conflicting beliefs literally clashing into each other. The physical result is that our bodies fall or crash into other physical objects. It is a way our body consciousness tries to wake us up to ourselves. A safer, yet still physical, way to wake up is via the body-mind therapies.

These therapies are particularly effective in assisting clients stuck in intellectualism. Having the person not talk or think about symptoms is step number one. Giving them a breathing exercise occupies that space and helps them to move their energy focus into the hara area energy centers.[3] If they are willing to sustain the deep breathing exercise for 20 to 30 minutes, then repressed emotions are freed to surface. In very fearful people, it's a big if. Most can not do it without practicing and they usually need a very pressing personal reason to practice and continue therapy.

After sustained deep breathing has helped unfinished emotional business to the surface, then pressure points worked along the corresponding meridians can more fully awaken the emotion needing to be processed and healed. When a repressed feeling is experienced as it was and moves through the emotional cycle to what the person would like it to be, then its "power" is freed for the person to use positively. This process takes from about ten sessions to two years, or more, of body-mind therapy.

The impact of freed emotional powers is exemplified in the person who is able to equally love the physical, emotional, mental, and spiritual self. S/He is also able to empathize, i.e., be at-one, with plants, animals, insects, rocks, and all races of human beings. S/He grieves freely at the loss of any physical representation of consciousness such as endangered plants, animals, land, air, water, and other human beings. S/He knows "oneness" with All on Planet Earth and fears for her/his own annihilation as s/he sees Her beauty die. S/He then gets angry at the mistakes s/he sees brothers and sisters making that contribute to the unnatural and unnecessary destruction of nurturing resources. S/He takes a stand, using the energy of anger and declares love for All-That-Is. S/He then acts, out of personal version and vision of tomorrow, to change what is in her/his power to change. Through creativity s/he becomes one with All, the Goddess, God.

To attain this level of natural spirituality and harmonious flow of the emotions a person needs an intimate "knowing" of each of the emotions.

Chapter Five Notes

1. Roberts, Jane. THE INDIVIDUAL AND THE NATURE OF MASS EVENTS, session 857, May 30, 1979.

2. Roberts, Jane, THE NATURE OF PERSONAL REALITY, Seth session 633, January 17, 1973.

3. Hara is a Japanese terms. Loosely translated, it means the abdominal area. Volumes have been written about its deeper meaning. Hara is where our Power To Be resides. It is where the life force springs and nurtures all of the other systems in the body. It is where our childself lives.

6

Fear: The Courage To Change

I AM root chakra, the base from which arises the Kundalini and from which flows the essence of the life force. I am connected with the energies of bladder and kidney. I am Water Element. I flow, like rivers, in the arteries and out the veins of your very being. Like tides of liquid spirit, I flow into you giving you life, and out of you cleansing your physical being. I am the life force in liquid form. I am 97.6% of your body. And when, like a mountain stream, you are flowing with your emotions, I help you gather momentum for Courage to Change.

Winter is my entry point into your psyche. Winter is the time of year of incubation, hibernation and transformation of fluid into form, of semen and egg into embryo, of water into ice, and, the solidifying of two gasses: hydrogen and oxygen into substance. It is in Winter that Spirit readies itself to become, in the Springtime, physical form.

AFFIRMATION:
I am the waters of the oceans, streams, lakes, water falls, still pools, steam rising, gentle rain, delicate snowflakes, and flowing fluids of love.

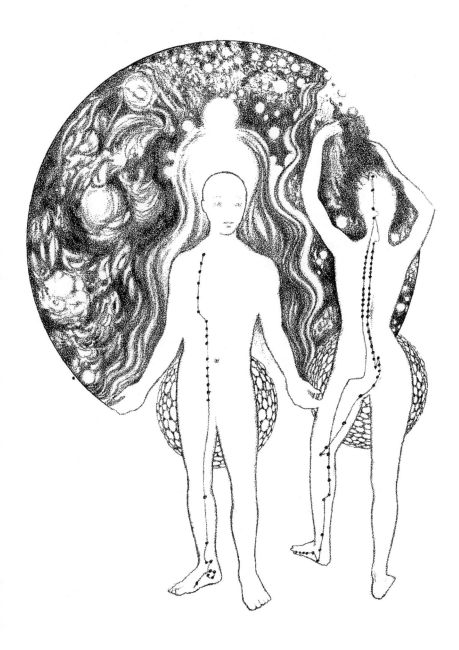

CHAPTER SIX

Fear: The Courage To Change

Fear, faced and felt
with its bodily sensations and the thoughts
that go along with it, will automatically bring about
its own state of resolution. The conscious system of beliefs
behind the impediment will be illuminated, and you will
realize that you feel a certain way because you
believe an idea that causes and justifies
such a reaction.

Seth
The Nature Of Personal Reality, Session 644,
February 28, 1973

F ear is the most debilitating and pervasively distorted of all
the emotions. More of my clients have chronically deficient
kidney/bladder meridians than any of the other meridians combined. A chronically deficient kidney/bladder energy signals the
following:

1)   Emotional abuse, in particular, not being wanted between
     conception and nine months.

2)   As a child, and then later as an adult, emotionally and
     intellectually operating out of a stance of feeling insecure
     and shamed for Being.

68

3) Believing and perpetuating the concept that love is
    conditional. "Only if you would...then I could love you."

4) Sexual energy distortions such as incest, rape, misogyny,
    and homophobia.

5) Having GREAT difficulty believing they can and
    consequently very seldom daring to try to make a living
    by doing what they love.

6) And most pervasively, choosing to perpetuate fear based
    systems out of the fear and the belief that humans and all
    physical life are basically evil.

All oral and sexual addictions originate from emotional wounds
incurred during conception to nine months. These include all
forms of substance abuse: food, drugs, alcohol, and nicotine; and all
levels of sexual addictions. All of these wounds begin in the womb
by a child knowing s/he is not wanted in physical form because
environmental conditions cannot provide a quality of life. When a
woman is pregnant, she is in a heightened state of awareness of the
mass consciousness of all beings. If she feels she does not want the
child, this is usually Mother Nature's way of telling her that there are
already too many children in the world and the mother is being
urged to lovingly say "no". Ancient cultures living close to the Earth
and the Goddess religions listened to this intuitive knowing and had
natural herbs for abortions, and natural forms of contraception to
preserve quality of life for their children and community. As Monica
Sjoo and Barbara Mor points out,

> *When women are in natural control of our own fertility,
> population is always kept in practical relation to the needs
> of the group and the abundance of the environment...But
> when contraception and abortion are not practiced, the
> results are even more extreme: infanticide, malnutrition,
> infant starvation deaths, mass famine. No woman, making*

her own choices, would deliberately bear children only to see them starve to death.[1]

Seth concurs and explains that modern day women also hear that voice via our conscious minds:

When women give birth in a crowded world they also know, and with a portion of their conscious minds, that a violation is involved. When your species sees that it is destroying other species and disrupting the natural balance, then it is consciously aware of its violation. When such natural guilt is not faced there are other mechanisms that must be employed. Again at the risk of repeating myself: Many of your problems result from the fact that you do not accept the responsibility of your own consciousness. It is meant to assess the reality that is unconsciously formed in direct replica of your thoughts and expectations. When you do not embrace this conscious knowledge, but refuse it, you are not using one of the finest "tools" ever created by your species, and you are to a large extent denying your birthright and heritage.[2]

When we are stuck in fear/denial then we do not value our bio-spiritual selves, nor the messages that our loving soul Self gives us via our conscious minds. Being stuck in fear separates us from a sense of security in our physical form and therefore separates us from Mother Earth who is the provider of our physical form. This in turn disconnects us from All That Is, and we feel shamed at the least slight.

Several years ago, columnist, Ann Landers did a survey asking how many parents would have children if they could do it over again. Seventy percent said they would not. More recent statistics indicate about 38 percent of parents actively participate in parent/teacher organizations, and that about 30 percent of families involving step children stay together. This could possibly indicate that the number of adults having children, that really want to have children, is only about 30%. The other 70% who have children do so for various reasons such as: social pressure: i.e., fear of doing something wrong, or fear of their religion's dogma if one uses contraceptives, or fear of revenge by God if one has an abortion, or fear that they aren't "good enough" so they unconsciously want to heal their own childhood by having a child through which to vicariously live.

When we have children that aren't consciously wanted and prepared for *before* conception we are inflicting an emotional wound that will effect generation after generation if not healed. As many healers of the inner child see it, 100% of us have been, at this point affected, either directly or indirectly, with this wound thus creating mass paranoia, and insecurity. This mass, unconscious insecurity is what keeps us, as a species, disconnected from fully realizing our biospirituality and Oneness with all other beings.

We, as a species, have much to heal. For adult children to transform this constant sense of insecurity— John Bradshaw calls it "toxic shame"–to "courage to change" takes a major "mind-over-matter" effort.[3] Being simultaneously courageous and fearful have to be given constant mental permission to co-exist. The child-self needs to hear and feel repeated gestures of compassion.

For example, it seems like "one hundred thousand" reassurances are needed to convince a person that loss of life or, an act of evil will not befall them if the child-self is allowed to express anger at a symbol (usually a pillow) of an abusive parent whom they feared so much.

The sense of emotional and physical security has been so damaged that the biggest challenge is to recognize how "shamed for Being" a person is feeling, and to own the feelings involved.

People in far less pain, yet who are in denial of their emotions have a poorer chance of learning to own and heal their feelings. People living out of fear hang on to old habits and old disconnected ways for a long time, often until they die. "When pain is all you know, it is your security blanket no matter how much it hurts yourself and others." If these people ever choose to heal in this life time, it takes lots of unconditional love from self and others daily to assist these child-selves to courageously walk through the "valley of the shadow of death".

At first, this is done intellectually. The laws of self-hypnosis, positive power of thinking, and repeated suggestions of success are effective in getting this boulder of fear to roll away from the tomb. Inside the tomb, the courageous discover it's really a womb leading to a rebirth of exuberance and passion for living.

This hypothetical tomb contains all the fears, self-doubts, and beliefs of unworthiness. This shows itself as toxic shame. Toxic shame is someone else's unowned feelings. Usually the parents, or other primary caretakers in a person's life when s/he was an infant. In the infant stage, the "I am you" stage, there is an unseen umbilical cord through which we absorb and cellularly record the feelings and beliefs of our care-givers. We are supposed to because it is through our care takers emotions that we acquaint ourselves with our new world.

The very core sense of God-self is connected with this psychological umbilical chord to the outside-of-ourselves world. If we are wounded in this stage, instead of unconditionally loved, we often may form very negative beliefs about life and easily get stuck in fear to change, which we carry into adulthood.

If we fear change and change anyway, a miracle happens. We stop fearing death. Joseph Chilton Pearce in his book, *Crack In The Cosmic Egg*, sighted two examples of what a person can do when she has transcended her fear of death. In both cases a woman's life was threatened by a violent man who had recently killed others. In both cases the women gave absolutely no energy to the possibility of death and instead, spoke to the man through pure compassion which comes from the womb of "being". It saved the women's lives because they were, in fact, willing to lose them.[4] Ultimately, any fear is a fear of death or evil. When a client is willing to go to the source of her or his fear, I have found that adult children emotionally abused before the age of five are very insecure and most often fear "not being loved". If they were more emotionally abused and shamed for Being from school age on they mostly fear "not being good enough".

Hillary was abused in infancy on through school age to the point of becoming suicidal in junior high. Hillary now exhibits multiple personalities and it is through them that she has discovered the sexual and physical abuse she experienced beginning in infancy.

Ironically, she still often denies the abuse because she is frozen in fear of what might happen to her if she were to defy the authoritative voice of her father, which she has significantly internalized. This internalized voice keeps telling her how awful she is.

"You're no good, and you're a liar," said with much contempt keeps her cowered into believing she's not worthy of even being alive.[5] Hillary is conscious of the different personalities as they present themselves and speak but then forgets and slips back into denying anything ever happened to her.

We've been working together intensely for two years now. Hillary first came to me about ten years ago. Between then and now she experienced many forms of psychotherapy, hypnosis, and psychoanalysis and returned to the hands on approach. We are making progress, although we cannot get to the point of integration until Hillary feels safe enough to stop denying what happened to her. Meanwhile, Hillary has translated her emotional pain into many physical ailments including chronic fatigue syndrome. She has about five different doctors that she sees regularly, continuously looking for one of them to cure her. As long as she is stuck in such great fear/denial, she will not believe that she has the power to be a well person and all the doctors in the world, including me, probably will not be able to help her.

Clients who believe they have the power to be well are the ones who move the most quickly through the denial and projection stages into owning one-hundred-percent-responsibility for their feelings. They also feel the most free to feel and express anger. As mentioned before, I use the ability-to-get-angry test to determine how stuck in fear/denial a person is. Then I know how short or long a distance we have to travel to the point a person is willing to take one-hundred-percent-responsibility for joy in his or her life. When a person is able to fully express anger, not just rage, and the beliefs about anger are positive, then reclaiming the power of the wonder child-self is eminent and is usually lasting.

The perpetuation of childhood wounds into adulthood is usually due to an unconscious decision made at the time the wound was incurred. The result is that the person attracts life-long reoccurring distorted experiences proving the decision to be true and valid. Eventually the body records these decisions as biological truths.

These distorted assumptions, over time, attach themselves with the first and second energy centers. Later in life these assumptions are experienced as "gut level truths", making it even more difficult to change the beliefs behind them. Since these decisions happen before a child is fully conscious of physical life, yet are recorded in the cellular memory banks, then a return to infancy and non-verbal forms of communication, such as touch, are paramount in affecting healing.

Adult children reared with the threat of punishment or any form of abuse, are subject to this deeply ingrained fear through which they view life. Since it is their most familiar way of viewing life, many, unfortunately, seek out, or stay enmeshed in religions that preach the existence of evil, and other organizations or scenarios that perpetuate prejudice and punishment. Thus the victim, persecutor, and rescuer cycle feeds itself from one generation to the next resulting in millions and millions of people, with very scared children inside them, supporting the very institutions that perpetuate their being stuck in fear.

Two outstanding symptoms of a person whose child-self is stuck in fear are:

1)   Intolerance of views different from his or her own.

2)   Refusal to hear what another person is really saying. This

refusal often turns into a disability to hear, and/or other hearing impairment. This is not true if a person is born deaf, but of people who become deaf over time either from disease or accident due to great fear.

The two above symptoms feed each other. A person who is too scared to tolerate another way of thinking will automatically "mishear" what another is saying and simultaneously reinforce his or her intolerance. All of our racial, social, and sexual prejudices are examples of the millions of people whose child-selves are stuck in fear. We are truly a planet full of fearful, very emotionally abused children. Like any frightened, backed into the corner animal, these child-selves often try to compensate by lashing out at the world by being physically and verbally violent or highly competitive. The need to be in control is also a stance taken by the fearful and is reflected in individuals' and institutions' many "rules and regulations" which indicate a severe lack of trust in their own and other's innate goodness.

We have about 2,000 years worth of rules and regulations aimed at controlling Nature, which is the archetypical example of the emotions on our Planet. The attempt to control Nature instead of living in harmony with Her originated as a political tactic to transform God's laws in Nature to man's laws over Nature. Nature has always been referred to as feminine. In the days of revering agriculture and the feminine, God and Nature were one in the same, and they still are. We have simply forgotten.

Included in living in harmony with Nature is natural reverence for sexual energy. The farther away we are from living spiritual sexuality the more abusive and perverse are our sexual acts. Harsh rules and regulations lead to abuse of sex. Having loving sex exemplified as a family attitude creates spiritual sexuality. We are naturally sexual beings. If we weren't divinely meant to be sexual we would not have sexual parts and loving, spiritual sexuality would not produce the ecstatic state of consciousness that it does.

Other, or altered, states of consciousness are a bio-spiritual *need*. It is not a coincidence that all of the addictions attributed to the first energy center alter consciousness. They are all attempts to re-create the loving, altered state of consciousness produced when we, as babies, should have experienced the ecstatic state of being unconditionally loved, via the loving touch and sound of the adult human caring for us.

Women who love being mothers, and men who love being fathers, *do* pass this sense of ecstatic security on to their children. These are the parents whom Nature intended to rear children. Paradoxically, all forms of sexual abuse and addictions are uneducated and distorted attempts to heal what a person's wounded childself never got in the "I am you" stage of development. (See the Emotional Energy Development Chart on pages 18-19)

Sexual energy is a million times more than getting the juices running and having intercourse. It is directly connected with the first (root) and second (womb) energy centers. In all of the ancient teachings of Oriental and close to Mother Earth teachings, sexual energy is directly connected with our life force. In Chinese, it's called "chi" or "qi". In Japanese, it's called "ki". In Native American tradition it's called "orende". Whihelm Reich called it "orgone". Eastern Indians call it "prana". The point is, globally, and for thousands of years, sexual energy has been recognized as our direct line to our "life force" energy.

When we are stuck in fear/denial, or when our conception through nine month needs have not been met, or when we are taught that our elimination functions are dirty or not as important as the spiritual act of eating, or when our sexual selves are taught to us as separate from our spiritual selves, we are setting the stage for violation and abuse of the self, and all other beings.

When New Age teachings emphasize raising the energy up out of the lower energy centers, instead of healing the wounds of these centers and emphasizing their energy and beauty, they are teaching perpetuation of the great rift between our emotional, sexual,

76

spiritual, feminist, and intellectual selves. The "life force" is directly reflected in the kidney meridian energy. Kidney "yin" energy deficient not only means the six adverse effects listed at the beginning of this chapter, it also means the life force energy (essence) line to our very Divinity is being drained, weakened, and/or killed due to continuation of the great rift we individually and as a species have created.

Prolonged kidney "yin" energy deficiency signals proportionate disconnection of the direct line of our physical bodies to God/Goddess/All-that-Is. As a species, I feel we can no longer afford this disconnection of ourselves from all of Nature. These next few years are opportunities to heal these very wounded child-selves in each of us, and to re-instate trust in our innate spirit-made-flesh goodness. Trust, in our innate goodness, is reflected in the Wonder-child in all of us. Among the many attributes of the Wonder-child is natural, loving, spontaneous compassion.

Chapter Six Notes

1. Sjoo, Monica, & Barbara Mor. *The Great Cosmic Mother: Rediscovering the Religion of the Earth*, p. 200 & 201.

2. Roberts, Jane, *The Nature Of Personal Reality*, Seth session 633, January 17, 1973.

3. John Bradshaw has several books and TV lecture series that I highly recommend. They are listed in the references. I interpret toxic shame as "other people's unowned emotions." Judgmental and critical statements are most often being spoken out of the voice of "toxic shame."

4. Pearce, Joseph Chilton, *The Crack in the Cosmic Egg*, pgs. 264-268.

5. On either the Oprah Winfry or the Donahue show one severely sexually abused young woman said that the "emotional" abuse did the most damage to her. Being told, from a very young age, that you are no good, etc. abuses the very soul of a person.

7

Compassion: The Hub Of Emotional Balance

I AM the womb chakra, in you whether you ar man or woman. I nurture all of the other chakras through your stomach and spleen (pancreas) meridians. I am the center out of which the umbilical cord of compassion links summer with fall, fall with winter, winter with spring, spring with summer, and you with all other consciousness.

I am Earth Element and my heart beats the sound of drum-drum, drum-drum, drum-drum. Just as the leaves of trees take in your carbon dioxide and out of it make oxygen, so do I absorb all feces and out of it make you Earth in which to grow food.

I am, therefore, the all absorbing, transforming, nurturing passion and compassion for all who live upon me—your Mother Earth. Over thinking and over eating dull my senses and disconnect you from me and all other creatures.

AFFIRMATION:
I place my hands on the belly of Mother Earth around my navel. I feel Mother Earth rise and fall with each deep breath I take. I feel Her nurture me when I breathe in. I feel her cleanse me when I breathe out.

Compassion: The Hub Of Emotional Balance

When you follow   your own nature,
you automatically and naturally feel for the needs
of others. When you are joyful and free, and when you are
having fun, you automatically, feel...your oneness with all
other creatures of the universe, and you know your place in
All-That-Is. And when you are yourself, others look
upon you with awe and joy and understanding
and you look the same upon them. And you
help every other creature that shares
with you the framework
of this Earth...

— Seth
Conversations With Seth, Vol. 1
by Sue Watkins, 1980, p. 206

T he ground work for a balanced sense of compassion is laid during the pre-toddler, I am you and me, stage of development. This is the stage just before the terrific twos. This is the stage where we go from crawling to toddling, from belly close to Mother Earth to bringing a conception of Her inside of us as we stand up-right and begin to walk.

Belly close to the Mother is our emotions naturally enmeshed with our parents emotions. Our emotional boundaries are naturally and healthily permeable membranes experiencing and exploring the feeling tones of other humans and other species. A basis for our kinship with all our relations—the mineral and plant sisters and brothers, Father Sun, Mother Earth, and all the loving, nurturing spirits that are always with us in the wind, rain, snow, hot, and cold—is established at this time.

This is when we internalize the womb of Mother Earth into our second energy center that becomes our wombs of compassion for All-That-Is. This is when we notice what our parents love and value most. Where we feel the greatest amount of energy being focused by our parents is where we also begin to focus our love in order to connect with them.

Shortly after the child begins to walk and talk with confidence, i.e., when the "I am me" stage is established, then the child will begin to reflect what s/he senses the parent loves. If the child scolds and criticizes that is where s/he is interpreting that the "love" energy goes. If the child plays cooperatively, lovingly, and respectfully, then that is where s/he observes and interprets the "love" energy is focused. One child I know has talked incessantly, since he began talking, about tractors. His father is a farmer and puts a great deal of time into the farm machinery. So, the child learns to connect with the love of the parent via what the parent appears, to him, to love; "I am me" looks just like Daddy.[1]

This is the age, nine months to two years, at which we are laying the foundation for compassion, or not, that will begin to be expressed as soon as the child starts talking. How s/he will treat him or herself and all of his or her sisters and brothers, regardless of species, takes root at this time. And we, the adults, are the role models and teachers.

This is the age humans begin to develop our naturally sensitive selves. Projection and reception of consciousness is a natural attribute and awakens at this time. If a parent has a wounded child inside, then abuse of the next generation becomes external and obvious at about the time their child is entering the toddler (I am me) stage—age two through three, and the disconnect cycle begins again.

The abuse comes in the form of adults imposing their beliefs— should's and have to's—on the child that is beginning to demand his and her own rights. Displays of anger and temper tantrums occurring at this time are taught as "bad". This is the abuse. The next chapter offers a new view of the use of anger i.e., natural aggression.

To foster a healthy, natural sensitivity, many hours need to be spent with the Great Mother—Mother Earth, at this age of development. In cultures where the parents are close to the natural world, they exude a oneness, a deep peace, an alertness to the surroundings, a connectedness with the food they eat, the clothes they wear, and a sacredness that is the Great Mother: this is important at this time because this emotional bond with nature is what the nine month to two year old resonates with and internalizes perhaps the rest of his/her life. When it is not there, when spankings occur instead of connectedness, and when should's and have to's over-ride natural belonging, the child retreats to the first energy center where s/he gets stuck in an exaggerated fear of this world. This is especially detrimental to a child who has a strong tendency towards retaining sensitivity. Johann showed me what this can lead to.

Johann was a sensitive who, the last time I saw him, was stuck in fear and anger, including other people's. He and I were among 80 participants in an emotional, mental, and physical intensive. We had all chosen this 17 day outdoor experience in order to push ourselves to our limits. Under a huge tent we had group gatherings for various classes and experiences. There were at least five psychotherapists as part of the teaching team, so I knew that whomever needed extra attention in our group would get it. But, as Johann stood telling his story, I could feel the energies flying. He began to tell his story then he hesitated, looked down, and it looked to me like he was gathering the groups fears and angers and becoming overwhelmed. He was very telepathic and knew that some people were thinking he was mentally ill. He even said so to the group. When he did, many went into denial of their feelings and they (the energy from the unowned feelings) began to fly around. The strength of emotional energies was so high, I could see them pass back and forth between Johann and certain people in the group. Johann became very agitated and soon withdrew, taking with him several other peoples' angers and fears. I could actually see these people rest back into themselves with relief.

A few days later, there was an incident with Johann in which he threatened to kill several people and was, therefore, asked to return to an outpatient home where he had been receiving treatment for his paranoid sensitivity. I do not know the precise diagnosis of his condition.

A week later he was allowed to return. The previous week, on the day of the group gathering in which Johann had become so agitated, I had been wearing a plaid shirt with the exact same print he was wearing. He now walked up to me and said, "You know, while I was gone, I almost did something awful, but then I remembered how calm and peaceful you felt in your shirt that looks like my jacket and I became you for a moment and didn't do the awful thing I was going to do."

Johann and I did not know each other, other than the energy exchange during the group gathering and those few words he spoke to me that day, but the impact he had on me woke me up to the many times I had felt other's feelings and had thought they were my own.

Sensitive people like Johann and many, many others, display the following:

1) An ability to know what you are thinking and feeling, even when you say just the opposite. (Granted, it sometimes gets twisted around according to the sensitive's emotional state and beliefs.)

2) An ability to act out *your* feelings because their compassion level is so high.

3) An opposite and equal ability to completely disassociate from all feelings, especially their own, and to go into trance, another personality, or appear catatonic.

4) They can also "read" the emotional atmosphere, at varying radii, and appear paranoid if they tune themselves to only detecting and/or projecting fear, which they most often do.

5) They can "voice" the emotions and thoughts of others by allowing their emotional boundaries to so merge with atmospheric emotional/thought energies that they lose contact with their own.

Done by sensitives, also called "psychics" these abilities have other names: (corresponding with the above)

1) Telepathy

2) Shamanism

3) Projection of Consciousness

4) Clairsentience

5) Channeling or mediumship

In all cases, if not before, then during the development of these abilities, very sensitive people will often experience their emotions in depth and go through periods of paranoia, schizophrenia, and other neurosis. The difference between a healer/shaman/Christian mystic, or other mystic, and a person labeled as paranoid, schizophrenic, emotionally unstable, etc., is that the emotionally functioning sensitives don't get "stuck" in the emotional depths of fear, grief, sadness, or anger. The chronically emotionally unstable do. Yet, sensitives may at times appear, and be, very emotional.

The experience of the shaman and the Shakti woman, as Vicki Nobel calls the modern shamaness, best describe the emotional process of delving into the world of the emotions and coming back out unscathed.[2]

Richard Noll, while a doctoral candidate in clinical psychology and a psychologist at Ancora Psychiatric Hospital made the following observation about the difference between shamans and certain inmates at the hospital:

> *Shamans "see" and "talk" to spirits; schizophrenics and other psychotics "hear voices" of spirits and sometimes "see" or "feel" them when they "shouldn't." What's the difference?...Volition is the key difference: the shaman actively seeks out the spirits in deliberately induced altered states of consciousness, which is only a part-time activity, as he must maintain full social and occupational functioning. The person undergoing a psychosis is victimized by the voices,...*[3]

It is the path of the shaman that most parallels and explains my own experience:

THE PATH OF THE SHAMAN	MY EXPERIENCES
1. Around the age of 6 or 7 signs of a potential shaman are looked for in children in cultures that have shamans.	1. In the 50's before we knew how terrible DDT was, we used it on our farm. As a result we had several kittens born with front feet frozen in a bent position. I seemed to know what to do and healed several of them so they could walk normally. I was about six years old. At about that age the wolf first appeared in my dreams. S/he chased me under our outdoor clotheline, into the house and up to the attic. Then I woke up.

2. At about puberty another natural initiation occurs. Either a physical disease, or an emotionally challenging situation occurs that is life or sanity threatening. In cultures that foster shamanism, vision quest types of experiences may be staged that produce a life or sanity threatening situation. Either way, this threat seems to stimulate communication with spirit world.

2. At age 15 I was diagnosed as having tuberculosis. Shortly after the diagnosis I had an experience with the aurora borealis that reassured me I would get well. Then at age 18 I was in a car accident that temporarily left me blind. For two years after that every time I put pressure on the back of my head I saw faces, in color, that many years later I would learn were like the faces of the Kachinas. I had the opportunity to tell a Hopi man about my experience. He said, "The Kachinas came to heal you."

3. The calling is circular, not linear. The spiral having begun in childhood and continuing through dreams, diseases, and traumatic experiences, or by formal training with another shaman, either from here or from spirit world. There is a point of no return in which an initiate must chose to, or not, to become a shaman:

Tribal people who practice shamanism, like the Huichols in Mexico, believe that a person will become ill and experience disastrous events in her life if she breaks her vow on the shamanic path to completion. The contract is between the person and Nature, so there is no easy way out of it, writes Vicki Noble in Shakti Woman.[4]

3. The final calling came for me shortly after my father's death. During a massage, and instigated by doing the ujjayi breath, I took my first volitional trip into spirit world. (See appendix I for a recount of the experience.) It was comparable to a near-death-experience. Five years later at a workshop with Dr. Marilyn Rossner, I experienced my second volitional trip into spirit world. This trip was not a result of trauma which gave it more validity for me: Two people were there to greet me. A long, grey haired Indian with a T-shirt on sat up out of a grave and told me he was dead but that I was not, therefore I should not be talking to him. (He became my teacher.) The other was a woman in an insane asylum. She had shoulder length bushy dark hair. She said she'd been there 40 years, since age 20. She was very glad to see me. She said she was psychic not crazy and that my work would now vindicate her. After that no matter what I went through I knew I wasn't crazy.

4. Death/rebirth and communication with the deceased and ancesters in what the German psychologist, Holger Kalweit, calls the "Beyond" is a common everyday occurrence and life-long theme in the life of a shaman:

...researchers into death and dying have compiled thousands of near-death experiences of modern people who have left their bodies as a result of accidents or severe illnesses. All these accounts of revived patients exhibit the same patterns and motifs that characterize shamanic odysseys to the beyond.

...One thing is certain, and this has been conveyed by all the accounts of those who have 'come back': The journey to the realm of the dead is the ultimate step in all therapies, the source of health and healing power, the highest goal of all the old religions as well as of our modern transpsychic and transphysical consciousness research.[5]

4. At age one month I almost died. Thereafter I yearly had life and death bouts with pneumonia. I remember being rushed (2 or 3 times) in the middle of the night to the home of our country doctor because I had stopped breathing. Since childhood I have displayed the symptoms of a near death experiencer. P.M. Atwater says that after a near death experience, *There is no avoiding psychism."[6]* Her research also shows that, *Survivors usually become quite sensitive to their surroundings and to other people. Everything expands while taste, texture, sounds, and feelings become unusually acute. Some sensitize evben to the point of becoming empaths, taking into themselves the pain, feelings, illnesses, joys, and conditions of others.[7]*

The desire to expand, more commonly called, "alter," consciousness is a natural biological need. Being in an altered state of consciousness is required in-order to empathize with another being whether human or another species. But, when our boundaries are violated in their developmental stages we learn to disconnect from ourselves and others' feelings and needs. In other words we learn to disassociate from our innate sensitivity and natural empathy.

When we heal the disconnects and repair the boundaries we reawaken our abilities to be the naturally compassionate beings we are meant to be. Balance in compassion is a function of the Earth Element, the second chakra, the womb, the child-self. It's external symbol is planet Earth. The condition of the Earth presently reflects the degree of disease in the womb and child-self of every human being. The pollution, over population, daily extinction of other species, breast and uterine cancer, show us that Mother Earth is in need of humans healing themselves emotionally so that they may be able to empathize with the environment in which we live.

We are Mother Earth and it is no coincidence that so many people are experiencing crash courses such as near death experiences (pun intended), healing the child within, spiritual experiences when loved ones die, training in shamanism, spiritualism, transforming illness, and any other situation that leads to experiencing an expansion of consciousness thus reawakening our ability to be in at-one-ment with All-That-Is. Healthy anger, Seth calls it natural aggression, is the fuel for that change.

Chapter Seven Notes

1. There is one other very important factor in operation here. I am convinced, because this child loves tractors and other farm machinery so much, that he came here, this life time, precisely because of his father's love for the same. If, however, this child does not feel unconditionally loved, this innate life's pleasure could later be an addiction he uses to avoid feeling his emotions.

2. I highly recommend *Shakti Woman, Feeling Our Fire* and *Healing Our World* to any woman who senses she may be a shaman. I dare say it's a "must read" if you haven't already.

3. Noll, Richard, *Shamanism*, Compiled by Shirley Nicholson, p. 54 & 55.

4. Nobel, Vicki, *Shakti Woman*, p. 82.

5. Kalweit, Holzer, *Shamans, Healers and Medicine Men*, p. 45.

6. Atwater, P.M.H., *Coming Back To Life*, p. 89.

7. Ibid. p. 90.

8

Anger:
The Power
To Be

I AM the source of your Power to Be You. If your sense of security center (first chakra) and your emotional boundaries (second chakra) are balanced, then I will be also.

I am the Wind in your sails and the illumination that arises in the East with the sun at dawn. I am the power that moves your muscle and gives your eyes sight to see.

I am liver that cleanses your blood and makes you new cells. I am the gall bladder that distributes your energy in directions you want it to go.

Affirmation:

I am that I am. I am naturally biologically divine. My likes and joys are my gifts to all humankind. The gift of who I am enriches all other life on Mother Earth and the Universe.

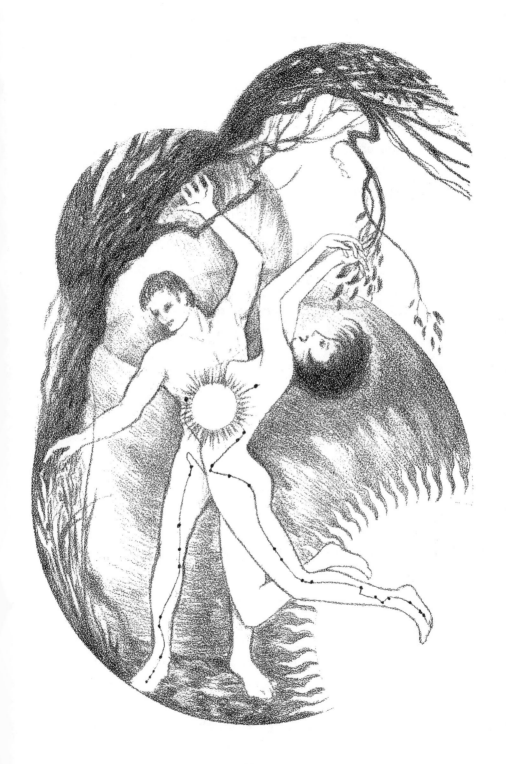

Anger: The Power To Be

"Natural aggression provides the charge for all creativity. Now reading this, many readers will be taken back, for they believe that love is the impetus, and that love is opposed to aggression. There is no such artificial division."

"Birth is an aggressive action—the thrust outward with great impetus of a self from within a body into a new environment. Any creative idea is aggressive."

– Seth
The Nature Of Personal Reality
Session 643, 10:45pm & Session 642, 10:28pm

I just don't see what good it'll do if I express anger," the client told me for the third session in a row.

"Then pretend you are angry and pound this pillow and yell. If there is no festered anger inside then the exercise will just be a miniature aerobic workout for your arms and lungs," I calmly told her.

"It won't do me any good to be angry," She replied, but I could feel she was holding onto festered anger. Her body signified it by having to be in control of every meridian stretch I tried to place her in. After much discussion it became clear that Madeline believed that being angry was bad, i.e., evil. She denied being afraid to express anger and again stated she simply didn't see any sense in it.

She heard about her need to express her festered anger from her psychotherapist, nutritionist, and chiropractor. She exercised regularly and ate a balanced and nutritious diet. She religiously listened to healing tapes and did everything her oncologist told her. She died a few months before her 49th birthday.

I felt both sad and angry that Madeline didn't get well. But, according to Seth,

> *No one dies under any circumstances who is not prepared to die. This applies to death through natural catastrophe as well as to any other situation.*[1]

Since death is as much a part of life as birth is, then it is logical to conclude that we can prepare for it just as we prepare for birth. As I explored my sadness and anger, I learned that what I was really angry about was that Madeline, in my opinion, had not chosen to fulfill her purpose here on Earth.

Then I began to realize that if "no one dies who is not prepared to...," then perhaps she had fulfilled what *she* wanted to do here. And I began to feel a deeper respect for people choosing what they want to do with their own lives.

Several years ago, when I was reading about circadian rhythms I read about a study concerning time of year deaths occurred. Of note to me at that time was that when people died of old age, with no major disease or accident as cause, many died in the Spring time just when Mother Earth is rebirthing herself. This suggests to me that when we die more consciously and naturally, many of us like to use the anger energy of Spring time in order to "spring" ourselves into the next dimension.

In fact, the ancient Oriental wisdom of the Five Elements teaches that the liver is the harbinger of the soul.[2] It's season is Spring, when all of nature is being reborn and its healthy emotion, anger, suggests that the thrust of a plant to burst out of the ground and our urge to be renewed each Spring is in the essence of this healthy energy called, "anger," or "natural aggression" as Seth calls it. It is the ability to feel anger and the use of it to define our boundaries that is its gift toward being self-actualized.

Anger is a rebirthing energy in our daily lives. Without it we can't say "no." Nor do we consciously know what our preferences are. When we don't know what our preferences are, and honor them, then we often put ourselves into victim roles, or other roles that sacrifice the very reason for being who we are. As one of my favorite teachers once said, "If you can't say no, your yeses don't mean much."[3]

The ability to express anger seems to be the deciding point between staying stuck in illness or some other victim role and becoming self-actualized. Adults who have been powerless victims of abuse in childhood have an especially hard time expressing anger even when it's only pretend. They, first of all, believe it won't do any good. The experience of powerlessness against an adult authority figure is firmly encoded in their child-self memory banks. Secondly, they made a childhood decision at that time that they were to remain in a powerless stance throughout their lives because they were, somehow, not good enough.

I hear two fears most often silently expressed by the child-self, during a session, when we address beliefs about expressing festered anger. One is, "I'm afraid I'll be annihilated if I change." The other fear is particular to most of the men and some of the women, "I'm afraid I'll be out of control with my festered anger and hurt somebody." The first fear ultimately is a fear of death of the self, and a deep need to feel unconditionally loved. The second fear, of killing someone else, suggests to me that the person is very aware of many years of accumulation of festered anger. Ironically, as a person approaches being able to express festered anger the fear of dying or killing someone else gets stronger.

What categorically has to happen is the victim-role self has to die and/or the persecutor symbol has to be annihilated in order to free the entrapped spirit-self to Be. This happens by momentarily losing conscious control of oneself, and relying on the physical and emotional consciousness, i.e., trusting in an innately good self that won't hurt self or others. That innately good self is a direct result of feeling unconditionally loved.

Without exception clients who cannot express their festered anger have stayed stuck in either illness or a victim role in life. Many have gone on to become terminally ill. "If I'm no good, why live?" is the unconscious reasoning of this person. When a person does not feel the benefits of feeling unconditionally loved–basic security and self esteem, the level of self worth is so low that self-destruct mechanisms click into action.

In contrast, those who do express festered anger to the emotional pitch necessary to affect a biochemical change within their bodies go on to do what they want to in life. When I see them, they are beaming with an inner joy and they look physically radiant.

A mountain of festered anger, built up over a life time, is best taken out in a conducive atmosphere and not on the person or persons a client is angry toward. A basement room, or an old shed can be set up to be the "anger release room". Newspapers to tear up, hand towels to bite or wring, pillows to kick and pound, an old mattress or a six inch thick futon, double bed size, on which to throw a tantrum are wonderful props to use to release "mountains" of festered anger. Throwing old bottles against a basement stone wall with a drop cloth underneath can also be an effective release. The point is to have something available that serves as a physical outlet for expressing anger. *Anger will not fully release unless it is done so physically and verbally simultaneously.*

Vigorous sports such as football, tennis and other competitive sports provide a temporary outlet, but they do not address the festered anger on a deep enough level. To process this kind of anger to completion and to focus on the intent of transforming festered anger into compassion for one's self involves taking progressive steps (given later in this chapter), which lead to discovering the emotion that is really lying underneath the anger. Festered anger is

95

very often a cover-up for deep fear, feeling not loved, and or grief for loss of what might have been.

Healthy anger helps us define our boundaries. It points out our likes and dislikes, which we are entitled to honor. When we don't honor them we are selling out a natural channel to passion for living. We are also disrespecting ourselves and lying to others about who we really are. Anger reminds us what our natural preferences and gifts are. It is the path that points out our bliss in life. Joseph Campbell is emphatic about it. About the man who has never followed his bliss, he says:

> *You may have a success in life, but then just think of it — what kind of life was it? What good was it — you've never done the things you wanted to do in all your life. I always tell my students, go where your body and soul want to go. When you have the feeling, then stay with it, and don't let anyone throw you off.*

Only when anger is repressed, believed to be evil, and repeatedly pushed into the liver and gall bladder does it become gall stones, liver diseases, stop purifying the blood, and turn into violence either toward self or other. Each time we hold back using anger as a power source to clarify our preferences and boundaries, we are adding fodder to an eventual volcano of festered anger. Some volcanos spew off a little everyday but because the person believes it is "bad" to be angry the volcano is fueled and ready to go the next day from new repressions. The eruption doesn't get to the point of emptying the volcano so that the person can see what is underneath it.

If s/he did s/he would probably find a child-self that feels so unloved and insecure that it believes it has to fight everyday for survival. This person has great difficulty relaxing during a session and is usually very armored with tight, hard muscles. Shiatsu is usually very painful for this person. Substance addictions are rampant and eventually this person develops heart problems.

Spouse abuse and child abuse cases attest to Seth's statement,

If you cannot express anger, you cannot express love. Not only that, but you get the two confused![5] Abuse crimes are most commonly committed by someone who supposedly loves the victim. Or, at least, would like to love him if s/he only knew how.

What are so many abusers angry at that they beat up and/or sexually abuse their own loved ones? Their child-selves are angry that they were not loved and don't know how else to express it. At an early age they learned to misbehave in order to get some form of love. Without touching we die. Misbehaving is a survival tactic.

Receiving a spanking is better than no touch at all. Soon this person learns that he gets "love" by doing violent acts. Roll this dirty snowball over from one generation into the next and we end up with what we have today: the majority of western families are emotionally dysfunctional, one out of every four women in our country is sexually abused, and a child is being beaten every minute.

Even though so many people on Planet Earth are stuck in anger at this time, there is potentially an inherent opportunity, if the anger is owned, to move us, on a mass scale, into an age of responsible self-actualization and creativity. Owning the anger and processing it to completion are the keys to the doors of a more harmonious and creatively loving time in our lives and those of the future.

The turn around begins with the individual. To own your anger say, "I feel angry about..." Avoid using the word, "you". Use of you when owning anger can switch the focus from the anger to the person you are angry at. However, saying, "I am angry at you," does help a person stuck in denial to begin to own the anger. Because of so much support to not own and show emotions in our society, the first two steps are usually going to be denial and then projection, either onto someone else or onto one's own self via illness.

1) *Denial*: "I'm not angry," she shouted. Or calm denial may be expressed: When this is the case others around this person get furious for/at him/her.

2) *Projection*: using or implying the word "you" with an

emotional charge behind it. Many turn the projection
onto themselves and become ill in some way.

Most people are stuck in either denial or projection and being
stuck is a way we give our power away.
To identify and own the feeling begins a healing and empowering
process:

3) *Owning the feeling:* "I feel angry about..." fill in the blank
with the action you are angry at. If you feel a rage
welling up inside, or feel very tired, or feel a knot in
your throat or suddenly don't feel well, go to steps 4 & 5.

4) *Ask yourself these questions:*

❖ How old do I feel right now? (a childself age)

❖ Where am I?

❖ What is happening to me?

❖ What am I feeling?

❖ What decision about life did I make at that time?

These questions will lead you to what initially happened that
led you to decide to play a victim role at this present time
and in other similar situations.

5) Now, instead of feeling like a victim, fight back, i.e., get
angry.

❖ Show your anger physically and verbally. Yelling and pounding or growling and wringing a towel, etc. have to be done
simultaneously. If you are not doing both at the same time
then your body will be holding back from fully releasing the
festered anger.

❖ Release anger in this way until you find yourself raging,
seemingly out of control. Please know that you are in

control. Trust in your innately good self to see to it that you do not harm yourself or others. Providing a safe atmosphere, such as a futon mattress on which to throw a temper tantrum is a good way to prepare.

❖ Shortly after reaching the out of control point ask yourself, "What did I want from this person I'm so angry at?" Repeat the question, "What did I want from him/her that I didn't get?" It takes a minute, but the child-self will answer.

6) *Healing begins:*

❖ Proceed to give the child-self what she or he wanted, i.e., to be held and told how special she was, or to be praised and told how proud his father was of him, or whatever it is the child-self requests of you. Hug or lovingly touch yourself as you verbalize what your child-self always wanted to hear.

❖ Allow yourself to feel the comfort, love, and specialness of that attention. Make sure you feel it throughout your whole body.

❖ Repeat this procedure each time anger from the past somehow surfaces. Since we humans are so good at repressing, it stands to reason that all of the festered anger from the past isn't going to go away in one time of doing this. But, it will go away, if you so choose, and transform into love much like an artist chisels away a hunk of rock, a little at a time, to reveal its beauty in an artistic form.

At first these steps to completion may take a half-hour or so. Eventually they can be done in a matter of minutes, and with, perhaps, using just the "Ha" breath.[6] Doing these steps on a regular basis brings three intrinsic rewards:

1) They give you freedom to feel your feelings of anger.

2) They give you a way to release them.

3)   They leave you feeling more self confidence and control
     over your reactions to others.

An angry reaction to a boss in the morning can be taken home
and dealt with at night. The boss does not have to be confronted
through anger. If after releasing the anger and, perhaps, finding
your five year old child-self was the one really angry at Daddy always
telling you what to do, but never praising you, you may find that you
had superimposed your reaction to your father to the situation with
your boss. After processing and healing the pain of the past you
may find yourself seeing or hearing what the boss said in the
morning to be entirely different than what you had at first perceived.

In any case it frees you from reacting out of unhealed childself
wounds, and instead, lets your emotional reaction become an avenue
through which you travel to either completing unfinished childhood
business or discovering a dislike that does need to be discussed with
your boss. An adult-self expressing a dislike can be done maturely
and constructively.

Acknowledging our likes and dislikes as rights is essential to
self-worth. A sense of self-worth is entwined with a sense of personal
power to Be.

> *That is the source of physical life, the sense of power and
> action. When a man or a woman feels powerless, as you
> think of it, he or she will die.*   *— Seth.*[7]

Expressing our likes and dislikes without the emotional charge
of an angry child-self behind them is a creative and affirming
experience for all involved. "I like how this & this look, and how
about we add this...," said without anger or fear and without being
in anger's and fear's other forms, such as judgement and guilt,
invites cooperation and team work. Said judgmentally, it invites a
defensive stance or said with guilt, it invites a need to be rescued. In
both cases a feeling of one person being up and the other down in
life is invoked.

To end the game playing and build self-esteem, it takes practice. Affirming your likes and dislikes moves you into the bliss of creativity. Processing the festered angers makes it easier to be clearer what your likes and dislikes are. A self test to know if you still have unfinished emotional business from the past is whether you feel confidence and peaceful acceptance of what your likes and dislikes are. If you aren't clear in a situation, what your likes and dislikes are, there is probably a hurt child-self underneath needing attention.

A like or a dislike does not have a hidden or overt emotional charge. Your desires/wants in any given situation are clear. Trusting in your innate goodness and following your deeper wants and desires, (not addictive wants and desires) in life leads to self-actualization and value fulfillment. This kind of unconditional self love teaches us to respect differences and to be less critical, less judgmental and more compassionate about All-That-Is.

Chapter Eight Notes

1. Roberts, Jane, *The Nature Of Personal Reality*, Seth session 665, May 23, 1973.

2. Connelly, Dianne, *Traditional Acupuncture: The Law Of The Five Elements*, p. 33.

3. Class lecture by Denise Roussell, PhD., June 1984, at the International College of Spiritual & Psychic Sciences week long intensive.

4. Campbell, Joseph, *The Power Of Myth*, p. 118

5. Watkins, Sue, *Conversations With Seth, Vol. II*, p. 328.

6. The "Ha" breath comes up from the tail bone and is practically yelled out. In fact, yelling is sometimes a part of it. Doing a wood chopping motion is a physical action that can be used to accompany the "Ha" breath. Or, just making fists and hitting downward in the air will also work.

7. Roberts, Jane, *The Nature Of Personal Reality*, Seth session 663, May 14, 1973, 10:59 pm.

CHAPTER

9

Sadness:
The Power
To Love

IAM heart chakra – the
heart of the matter – I hurt when your
heart's not in it – I ache for unity
between emotions and intellect – I am
LOVE.

I am Fire Element, the fire that melds
your thoughts and feelings, the fire
that burns away the old and stirs your
desires of passion to create when logic
and intuition marry inside of you.

I am small intestine meridian that
assimilates life for you. When you
assimilate other than what you love, I
refuse to get much out of it, nor do I
absorb the nutrients like I am capable
of.

I am your blood vessels and your
lymph system "heat" energy, I protect
the heart and carry nutrients and waste
to and from every cell in your body.
Love all of me so that I may show you
how much I love you. I am laughter,
joy and fun!

AFFIRMATION:
My passion for doing what I love
radiates, renews, and enables me to
share who I really am with all on
Mother Earth. Through my heart I
give and receive a love that lives
beyond all time. I experience life
with childlike joy and wonder.

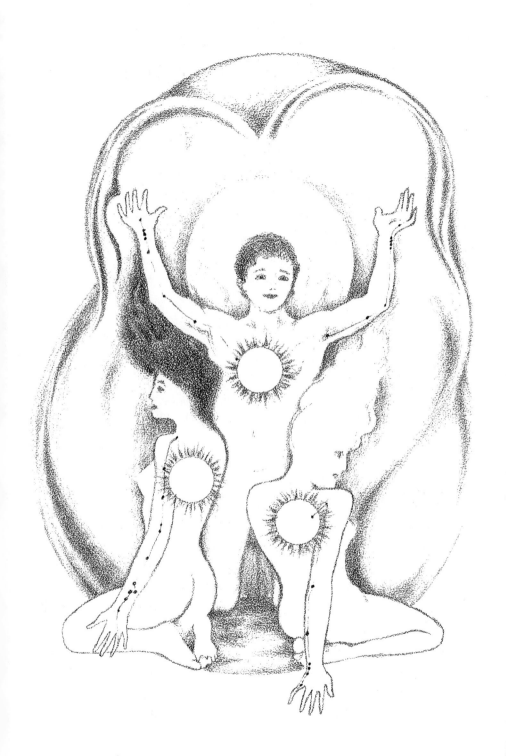

Sadness: The Power To Love

Love is a biological
as well as a spiritual characteristic.
Basically, love and creativity are synonymous.
Love exists without an object. It is the impetus
by which all being becomes manifest. Desire,
love, intent, belief and purpose—these form
the experience of your body
and all the events
it perceives.

— Seth
The Nature Of The Psyche: its Human Expression,
Session 792, January 24, 1977, 10:59pm

Week after week, three women clients in their 60's and 70's, who did not know each other, told me their tales of woe. They were negative tales of hopelessness and they were always about social issues. They seldom had much to say about their own aches and pains. Then it dawned on me one day, "these women really care!" Each had heart meridian jitsu, verified by them often talking throughout the session. Each was stuck in sadness and seeing only the pains in society. They especially loved nature and were most judgmental about what was happening to the environment. Their bellies were all big, rounded like the Earth and hard, indicating their second (emotional-self) and third (power to Be) chakras were also stuck and had been hardened by the times they grew up in: the depression and four major wars.

Yet, their individual powers to love had refused to die. They had merely hardened themselves into a focus of social sadness. These women were bitter and pessimistic because they loved so much.

Social sadness is often a means used by clients with heart jitsu to avoid dealing with their own emotional pains.[1] Ralph said that he always cried watching sad movies but he couldn't remember ever crying about anything in his own life. Men more than women clients reported this to be true for them. Perhaps the sitting and not doing fostered by the darkness of the movie theater or the safety of the home couch allowed the men a moment of feeling the emotions in the action of the movies because they were in a passive and receptive position in contrast to their daily focus in life.

Continually being stuck in sadness can eventually lead to heart kyo.[2] When incessant talking turns into an air of silent despair during the Shin Shiatsu session then this has happened. A kyo condition is more difficult to re-energize. Heart kyo can be a serious situation, especially if small intestine is jitsu. According to Dr. Shizuto Masunaga, a myocardial infarction can occur in the near future if these two meridians read this way at the same time.[3] A client is strongly encouraged to see her or his doctor, and the emotional tension of the body-mind immediately addressed. Since well trained shiatsu practitioners can detect very early signs of energy imbalance in the body, a client usually has time to change her or his stress load and help strengthen a weakened body-mind, thus reducing the chance of heart attack.

Childlike joy and wonder is how a healthy heart best expresses itself. A weakened body-mind and a constant negative outlook on life indicates a person has lost this childlike wonder. Problems with the heart and circulation will soon follow if the early symptoms are not heeded. What a person enjoyed doing as a child gives clues as to what s/he needs to be doing now to reawaken joy and wonder.

For instance, joyfully digging holes in a sandbox as a child, might be an indication the person would enjoy planting and seeing things grow as an adult. Or, putting on scarves, crowns and capes and presenting a play might indicate a person enjoys drama in some way. Or, if as a child, a person often pretended s/he was a shop keeper selling various items, this is quite likely preparation play for a future business that one would enjoy doing.

In cultures where shamanism is still practiced, a child is watched, at around the age of the change of teeth, to see what that child enjoys doing. Uncontaminated play, at this age, indicates what the future adult self will enjoy doing as a vocation. Thus, this play is seen as the gift a human being has come to this life time to give. From this age on until puberty this playtime enjoyment is gently encouraged by family and community.

Fourth chakra—heart chakra, "school age" development stage, solidifies the first, second, and third chakras. Free play, up until the change of teeth, while a child is still naturally sanguine, is vital to ensuring that the future adult self feels naturally loving and loved, and, feels secure in his or her values.

Honoring "likes," and a gut level sense of self worth can verify that an individual has an impact by simply Being. This fosters a belief in one's innate goodness and trust that by Being, a person will naturally, easily, lovingly/creatively, and cooperatively fulfill what s/he came to Mother Earth to do, i.e., LOVE.

The measure of love we live is directly reflected physiologically in our bodies. The first chakra in particular is effected. It's energy meridians are kidney and bladder. When we let fear rule a situation it creates an excess of Water Element energy. Water puts out the fire of love and passion for living. Fire element is composed of heart, blood, and small intestine meridians. Thus, an excess of fear, exhibited by kidney and bladder problems, squelches love: Assimilation of food (small intestine and blood circulation) gets upset. Appetite for food (second energy center function and sex (first and second energy center function) go off balance. The flow of the life force (function of kidney meridian) and creativity (function of the second energy center interacting especially with the first and third) become stagnant. Bellies harden, feces isn't eliminated as well as it should be, and we accelerate the aging process instead of the rejuvenation process.

The flowing of creativity and love is also tied in with seemingly mundane daily activities. Rearranging the living room, cleaning out the garage, or cooking a meal can reflect the status of creative wonderment of our hearts and body-minds. These activities can act as a meditation to show us if we are sad, or, in denial and avoiding feeling, or blaming someone or something else for what we feel, or in a creative and thus joyful state of mind. We need only listen to ourselves to find out.

We are given daily conscious clues as to the health of the heartbodymind. If your "heart's not in it" then you are stressing the body. Acknowledging these daily clues gives us the opportunity to choose what we want to do about them.

And, not everyone wants to go on physically living. When Annie ceased talking throughout the shiatsu session and her body-mind acted depressed and limp on the mat, I found her heart meridian to be very kyo. I gently asked her, "Do you want to die?"

"Yes," she replied, "nothing gives me pleasure anymore. My husband is gone. I've tried to be happy for two years now, and I'm not. I'm ready to go on."

"Do you have any unfinished emotional business with your family?" I asked her. "Are all your legal papers in order?"

"Everything is fine with my children. I've been trying to hold on for them but I'm not happy. And, my will and property are in order."

"And are you at peace with yourself about dying?" I asked with curiosity.

She smiled and calmly said, "I don't want to talk about it anymore."

Within the month, I heard she had died peacefully in her sleep.
According to Dr. Elizabeth Kubler-Ross and other death and
dying researchers, patients about ready to die and who are in the
acceptance stage don't have much to say anymore to the outside
world:

> *He wishes to be left alone or at least not stirred up by news
> and problems of the outside world. Visitors are often not
> desired and if they come, the patient is no longer in a
> talkative mood. He often requests limitation on the number
> of people and prefers short visits. This is the time when the
> television is off.*[4]

They are disconnecting from their family, friends, and physical
life. There is a calmness and inner peace in their demeanor that
bespeaks of a mystical beauty in their last moments. It is this display
of inner beauty that reassures me that death is birth. Death is a
major change of clothes in which we change our physical form as
well.

Perhaps the last moments of a person who is peacefully dying is
showing us that death can be a blissful experience, or, at the very
least, that physically dying can be pleasant: I wasn't present when
Dad died. Our wonderful country doctor said he was sitting with him
and talking to the nurse; he turned toward Dad to include him, and
he was gone. Obviously, he died peacefully, but, I had to see for
myself.

To the horror of the funeral home attendants, I insisted upon
seeing my father's body. "We haven't fixed him up yet," they
protested.

I began to fuss. My oldest brother could see I was determined.
"Let her see him," he commanded. So they did.

Either Dad somehow put a smile on his face, just for me, or, he
did indeed die peacefully.

It was very important for me to see him before they embalmed
him. It has given me great peace to see in his face that physically

dying was what Dad wanted, and that it was probably a pleasant experience.

When the fear of death and evil are minimal, space opens through which the child-self steps into a world of delight and wonder. Children who are happy and free to delight and wonder about the world, even death, are also able to be more clear about their likes and dislikes, and enjoy living more.

Besides reeducating our adult selves, The Waldorf school system is, perhaps, a ground floor from which we can teach the coming generations "respect for individual preferences and differences," and, at the same time, teach interracial, inter-ethnic, and inter-species cooperation, and, cooperative delight in uniqueness.[5] For when we honor our own likes and dislikes, we are more apt to honor the preferences of others.

What's okay and not okay in expressing likes and dislikes is developed during school age, the heart chakra development stage, and the interdependent stage of growth. If a child is told she or he is supposed to like everybody, or to dislike certain people, then he/she learns to discount his or her own feelings. This further teaches disconnect from one's innate self-worth and forces the energy unnaturally upward into the thinking realms. "Shoulds" and "have to's" are most strongly reinforced during this six year old to adolescent age.

Teaching a child to stay away from another child because he or she is of a different color, different religion, etc., teaches prejudice and bigotry. Children being cruel to other children, and children bullying other children are not natural behaviors. Very likely they are direct results of three factors:

1) Humans having unwanted children, who later on feel so insecure about their self worth that they feel they have to "fight" for it.

2) Prejudice and bigotry passed on by example of the adults in the children's lives.

3) Children not being allowed to live in their play and fantasy world until the change of teeth. Caroline von Heydebrand, 1886-1938, one of the great early teachers of Waldorf, speculated that children who weren't allowed the early childhood fantasies very possibly turned, later on, to the excitement of horror and violence. In her words (translated by Daphne Harwood):

Children who lack the vigorous nourishment of fairy stories, legends, mythology and vivid historical pictures seek nourishment elsewhere. Just as a hungry man who cannot find a morsel of bread will pick up rotten apples, and be glad to get them. Murder stories in the newspaper will then be read in secret, or a thrilling exchange of backstair stories will be carried on with school-mates. The rage for such reading comes on about the ninth year if the creative powers of the children have not been guided in the right way... [6]

Likes and dislikes are acted out in children's fantasies. Play time is very important for development of likes, and for learning to acknowledge others preferences without the burden of competition and comparison, which are learned, adaptive behaviors. If a pre-school offers the example of respect for differences and cooperation, a child naturally participates, especially if this respect is lived at home. [7]

If no other lessons but these are taught in grades one through seven, as well as at home and in our preschools, we would have a loving and cooperative world in which people would feel naturally secure, safe, and considerate of All-That-Is. This would free creativity and child-like wonder as well as interspecies cooperation which are innate tendencies in all humans.

But, we presently do not live these values. Is it any wonder heart disease is the number one killer of humans in the U.S.A? In shiatsu-energy terms it is because we keep forcing our body energy into the upper energy centers to comply to rules and regulations of an intellectually focused belief system that does not give emotional intelligence and childlike wonder equal validity.

It has been my experience that clients with heart meridian jitsu think far more than they feel. In fact, they work overtime controlling their emotions causing an overload on their heart energies. Unfortunately, it usually takes a major trauma to force them to let their energy drop into their feelings. Sometimes the heart just can't last that long and the conflicting beliefs cause any one of the heart related diseases. Many who are on specific diet and exercise programs to reduce the risk of heart disease still can't get their cholesterol levels down into healthy range. What keeps them forcing their energy upward into hypertension and the high incidence of heart ailments in this country? Perhaps it is fear of feeling and change which is a gut level activity. In order to transform this fake fear that drowns our love, we need to learn to grieve and let go, like a gentle rain, or a raging storm. This will help awaken our "wisdom to trust."

Chapter Nine Notes

1. Jitsu is a Japanese word meaning "excessive energy."

2. Kyo is a Japanese word meaning "lacking energy," in particular "ki," the Japanese word for life force.

3. Masunaga, Shizuto, with Wataru Ohashi, *Zen Shiatsu: How To Harmonize Yin And Yang For Better Health*, p. 157.

4. Kubler-Ross, Elisabeth, *On Death And Dying*, p.100.

5. Rudolph Steiner is the father of Waldorf and the philosophy of Anthroposophy. As I understand it, Waldorf encourages the individual talents and preferences of a child because it believes the child is naturally cooperative, naturally loving (sanguine), and, at the change of teeth, will naturally grow more academically focused. It further believes that up until the change of teeth, a child needs to live in the world of imagination and play in order to develop the body, mind, and spirit to be ready to handle the intellectual.

111

I would like to see a study done comparing the results of children reared in Waldorf as to how their experiences relate to the information of the development of the child used in humanistic psychology.

6. von Heydebrand, Caroline, translated by Daphne Harwood, *Childhood: A Study Of The Growing Years*, p. 84.

7. This phenomenon was observed during my four month assistant teaching experience at Red Rock Waldorf Playschool, Sedona, Arizona.

10

Grief: The Wisdom To Trust

I AM your first breath of physical life. I am your last goodbye breath when you physically die. I am unseen spirit that constantly links you with both the physical and spiritual world. I am the pathway through which all communication passes. Each breath you take communicates with all beings in all times. Each breath you give passes a part of me into other realities.

Through me you are always both living and dying, dying and being reborn someplace else. Your deadly carbon dioxide gives life to the leaf. The exhaled breath of a leaf gives life to you. I am the breath of life that constantly shows you there is no death.

I am Metal Element. I am the oxygen deprived or needed to transform minerals into beautiful forms you call gems and crystals. I am the residue given off from this transformation. In animated forms it is called feces or scat, depending on your species. For I am the breath and defecation you all share and communicate through.

AFFIRMATION:
I let go and trust. The sun assures me it will rise tomorrow. I let go and let All-That-Is Be. I am who I am and it is good.

Each death in Nature shows me over and over again that there is no death. There is only transformation.

Grief: The Wisdom To Trust

It is quite obvious that
people must die – not only because otherwise
you would overpopulate your world into extinction, but
because the nature of consciousness requires new experience,
challenge, and accomplishment. This is everywhere apparent
in nature itself. If there were no death, you would have to
invent it (smile) – for the context of that selfhood would be as
limited as the experience of a great sculptor given but one
hunk of stone (with quite dramatic emphasis).

– Seth
The Individual And The Nature Of Mass Events,
Session 803, 10:20 PM

Gail was 28 years old when her husband of two years con-
tracted a rare virus. It spread to his heart and in one
month's time he died. A few weeks later she started seeing a
psychiatrist who told her she needed to let go and get on with her
life. Emotionally, Gail was not ready to do that. She had unfinished emotional business with her husband and she wanted to
know him in his new life.

When Gail came for sessions she was angry at the psychiatrist
for telling her to let go of her husband. Underneath that, she was
angry at her husband for leaving her. "How could he do this to me?"

she asked me at our first session. In response I asked her if her father was dead or had left her in some way. Her parents had divorced when she was eight, she told me, and yes, she was angry at her father for leaving them.

Grieving the death of a loved one is a complicated matter because there is intense love and longing mingled with intense rage held down by extreme fear. Everything feels out of control. Yet, it is a most perfect time to heal wounds of the past because of the intensity of the emotions and because the wounds of the past are where the present situation began.

In the beginning sessions with Gail, the unfinished emotions from the past would clamber over each other asking for attention. I felt like I was trying to manage five children who insisted on all talking at once, at the same time using me as a jungle-gym. I suggested she attend a weekend intensive I offer called, *Awakening the Wonder Child Playshop.* A psychotherapist friend told me she felt our 16 hour intensive would save Gail six months of therapy.

During that weekend, Gail had a transformational experience. During a Gestalt-style conversation with her deceased husband, Gail experienced him touching her left arm, convincing her that he was indeed alive on an energy level. Depending on whether a person is more kinesthetic, visual, or auditory determines the method of having a mystical experience.

By physically feeling him, and believing it was her deceased husband, she was able to open up to communicating with him on a cellular level. She expressed her anger at him for leaving her and because she was convinced he was there with her, she was able to listen to his response and feel his love for her reassuring her that, yes, love goes beyond death and that this was the way it was supposed to be in order for both of them to fulfill their purposes.

If the qualities of the first three energy centers (sense of security, emotional boundaries, self worth) have not been developed to a functioning degree, not only do we have lots of heart problems, we usually also have a wounded child-self, (unhealthy fear, boundary issues, and poor self worth, for all of which we often use materialism or lack of, to compensate) and, a great deal of trouble trusting in the life-death-life cycle. When a loved one dies, our unhealed child-selves, Fear, Anger, and Grief can make us feel like some kind of emotional jungle gym! If we do not believe there is life after death, then we feel we cannot afford to get to know the loved one in a new light, so to speak. When we do not gut level believe in life after death, attempting to let go of the loved one magnifies all of our emotional childself wounds. A nagging usually unconscious longing arises for the repressed extraordinary skills we innately knew as children, i.e. talking with spirits etc.

In an attempt to reawaken these extraordinary skills, (it's at times like these that they are meant to be used) we may find ourselves heavily indulging in our addictions. To ease the pain of our unhealed emotional wounds that also come up at this time adds double weight to the indulging of our addictions. The oral, first energy center, addictions are especially stepped up: drugs, alcohol, cigarette smoking, drinking coffee, and sex, in particular. We naturally long to continue the relationship with the "love" of the deceased loved one. Our longing calls to them and they attempt to answer. They may show themselves to us in their new ghost-like form. Or, we might hear their voices calling us, even saying full sentences that are instantly transmitted to us telepathically. Or, funny things happen: objects disappear and reappear; the deceased's favorite cup falls off the counter and no one was anywhere near it to make it fall. Or a friend calls and says something to you, in terms not normally his or her jargon, but that your loved one used to say.

Transference is also a common avenue we choose to somehow perpetuate what we think we have lost. Usually this is done when the grieving person has lost a benevolent (or malevolent) authority figure. The new authority figure may be a counselor, another family member, or a friend with similar authoritative views to the deceased loved one. A person seeking or finding and then rebelling against

118

authority figures has a wounded school-age child inside. Thus, the grieving process is doubly painful.

But, when we cellularly and consciously know there is no death, then the natural grieving process is faster and healthier because it's less stressful and we have the opportunity to re-develop our abilities to communicate with spirit world. I say re-develop because we came into this world with this knowledge. The imaginary playmates, the sense of having a guardian angel when experiencing a crisis and hearing voices and feeling sensations of loved ones when we most need them, are the doorways into continuing a loving relationship with the deceased. A physician's assistant and Vietnam veteran told me this story:

I was a Marine and we were on patrol in thick jungle. I was the end person in the detail and it was dark. A few days earlier my best buddy had been killed. All of a sudden, and as clearly as you are hearing me now, I heard him say to me, 'Behind you! Swing your machete NOW!' I did and I killed a Viet Cong who was about to kill me. My dead buddy saved my life. [1]

For the most part this form of communication gets reawakened during a very traumatic event such as the above. The large number of core near death experiencers, has made this phenomena available to study on a major scale. Dr. Raymond Moody relates the following:

In several accounts I have collected, persons say that they had near-death experiences through which they were saved from physical death by the interposition of some spiritual agent or being. In each case, the person involved found himself (knowingly or unknowingly) in a potentially fatal accident or set of circumstances from which it was beyond his own powers to escape...Persons undergoing this relate that afterward their lives were changed, that they came to feel they were saved from death for a purpose. [2]

119

A sense of purpose in life combined with a gut-level knowing that there is life beyond this physical death frees one to more fully live.

There are natural, less traumatic and dramatic, ways to develop this trust and belief in life after death that is naturally available to us. We can begin by healing the child-selves in each of us and in our children before we create a major "crash" into this other world. The more aware we become the more obvious it is that every moment of change, in life, is teaching us the life-death-life cycle.

For instance, on a daily basis there are situations, events, and people we choose to let go for which we may only momentarily grieve. Even unpleasant situations require a gesture of letting go or grieving in order to be complete enough to make way for the new. For one young client, age eleven, it meant grieving the end of an abusive situation. How could she trust that what she was moving into wasn't going to be worse than what she was moving out of?

She had been on crutches for almost two weeks. Her left leg was in so much pain she couldn't put any pressure on it. The doctors couldn't find anything wrong. In a week, she was moving with her mother to a new state and a new life. Her father had been physically abusive. She had been unhappy at school except for one friend to whom she had already said good-bye.

"What are you feeling sad and powerless about?" I asked her as I connected lung (to grieve and to express) meridian pressure points with bladder (to flow with emotions) meridian points on her left, dorsal side.

"Mom hasn't asked me if I want to go...," she began to cry. She hadn't been included in on the decisions and felt she had no control. When her father was abusing her she also felt she had "no control". This is the logic of the emotions: even though her mother had provided the proper therapy and made several life style changes to save her daughter from further abuse by the father, the child within the child felt this as going from one "no control" situation to another. The emotions do not discern between good and bad situations. There are no polarities when one is in an emotional state.

At that point I asked her mother to come into the room. She was a psychotherapist and I suggested they, together, say good-bye to the old and make plans, together, for the new. I briefly explained my observation to the mother, knowing she would immediately understand. I left the room. One-half hour later they walked out of my office, the crutches were no longer needed.

Ceremonies of passage are very important to assist one through the grieving period. The ceremony can be as simple as verbally saying, "good-bye" or as elaborate as an event requiring a national mourning. The key to affecting ceremony of passage is the underlying sense of completeness with the person/people/species involved. Performing private ceremonies can make clear whether there is still more unfinished emotional business. Having a ceremony to help bring up unfinished business may mean having a final ceremony later on to finally, lovingly say "good-bye".

An at home, symbolic "burning" or "burying" ceremony is a physical act that further anchors a loving good-bye. Besides the socially accepted ceremonies of cremation or ground burial, private ceremonies of burning or burying token objects such as an article of clothing, also say good-bye to a deceased or lost loved one. Fire symbolizes transforming the physical into the spiritual or pure energy form. Without getting into personal religious and cultural beliefs, a person can experience a sense of completion through these private ceremonies. An awakened trust that there is a life after death is the result of a successful lovingly saying good-bye.

As Seth reminds us:

Dying is a biological necessity, not only for the individual, but to insure the continued vitality of the species. Dying is a spiritual and psychological necessity, for after a while the exuberant, ever-renewed energies of the spirit can no longer be translated into flesh. Inherently, each individual knows that he or she must die physically in order to survive spiritually and psychically. The self outgrows the flesh.[3]

When a person isn't ready to say goodbye, I suggest continued conversations with the deceased loved one. One may do this with both deceased four leggeds, i.e., pets, and two leggeds (human loved ones), with a resulting inner peace and inner gratification that we are indeed sharing the love that, since childhood, I "know" lives beyond the grave. Whenever I feel sadness for the lost loved one that is my cue to begin speaking to the deceased loved one as if s/he is present in the room.[4]

Feelings are the energy vector upon which deceased loved ones, including pets, can travel through the sense of no space and time. When we are in an emotional state we are in that same sense of no space and time. This is the womb-tomb-womb tunnel to the plane where we can mutually meet and share telepathic thoughts and love. It takes nothing more than shifting from focusing on the loss, to focusing on sharing love. It helps to talk out loud to the loved one whose presence you are sensing.

Then listen for a reply, or simply remain open to seeing or sensing their presence. It's a far more loving, soothing, and reassuring way to ease into letting go than feeling forced to abruptly say "good-bye".

Recently I had the honor of being a medium for a newly deceased mother of a very dear friend. I am always delighted, like a child, when something is said that has meaning to someone that reassures them or eases their pain. The statement was a simple one, "He better hurry up, because I have plans." The deceased mother was referring to her life-long companion, who was also dying. He joined her one week later.

Her daughter and granddaughters laughed, "Yup, that's Mom (Grandmom), she was always saying, 'I have plans...' "

Plans, dreams, purpose, meaning, are all benevolent forces that elicit our creativity. What would a world be like in which human beings were choosing to heal their emotional wounds, awaken their wonder child, take 100% responsibility for joy in their life, and gut level knew that we never died? Let's imagine.

Chapter Ten Notes

1. This man is scientifically orientated so I was really surprised when he shared this story. I never would have guessed...which says to me that there are probably a large number of people who have had experiences that they seldom, if ever, talk about. One study showed some 70% of all Americans have had some sort of experience with communication with deceased loved ones.

2. Moody, Dr. Raymond, M.D., *Reflections on Life After Life*, p. 159.

3. Roberts, Jane, *The Individual And Nature Of Mass Events*, Seth session 801, Apr. 18, 1977, 11:25 pm.

4. During the course of writing this book, my best friend died, my mother-in-law died, and our Great Dane companion of 8 and one half years died. All three of them were/are very dear to me. Continued conversations with them helped me truly know they continue to "live." Usually physical signs accompany the conversations. I always ask for some personal "proof."

5. Roberts, Jane, *The Nature Of Personal Reality*. Read Seth session 665 for more information about this.

11

Imagine

I AM inner vision. I am the sixth chakra–your third eye. I can see into your tomorrow and into your yesterday. I can see the geometric matrices being formed by your mass consciousness and mass beliefs. I am the blueprint of your creativity.

I am conception vessel. I am the yin aspects of your heart, kidneys, liver, pancreas, lungs, and blood vessels. I am the magnetic coming together of your heart's desire, your willingness to flow, your determination to Be, the chemistry of your being, your depth of breath and the vessels that connect all of these together.

Affirmation
I am that I am.

Imagine

*"What connects people
and separates them is the power of idea
and the force of imagination...Unless you think quite
consistently — and deeply — the importance of imagination quite
escapes you, and yet it literally forms the world that you
experience and the mass world in which you live."*

— Seth
The Individual and the Nature of Mass Events,
Session 829, 9:49 pm,
March 22,
1978

Everything in physical existence was first a thought, a dream, or an imagining. Without visualizing ideal thoughts and dreams in a less than ideal world, we would not have a better tomorrow to aspire toward. What would an ideal emotional climate in your world-view be like? I cannot create that fantasy for you. But, I can for myself and I invite you to join me. Let us go back to a time in childhood when we believed that magic was real, for it was then, perhaps, that you and I were at the height of our natural spirituality. This is my dream of tomorrow. In sharing it with you, I hope that it will stimulate you to create your own:

It is bedtime and I am four years old again. When I wake up in the morning everyone in the whole world is going to start owning their emotions. No one will blame anybody or anything outside of him or her self for personal feelings and circumstances. And, that very day, people everywhere will drop all law suits, stop all wars, stop all abuse of other human beings, other species, and themselves. They will begin to privately process their rage, heal their fear, and trust in the wisdom of their grief.

They know it will take time to transform their lifetimes of repressing feelings, blaming others, and game playing, but they are confident and feel supported because all societies on the planet are doing it. Asking for help from others who have made it before them—the self-actualized, the ordinary monks and mystics, and the blissful ones—will be an honorable apprenticeship and viewed by others as a sign of true resolve and true caring. Sharing the trying times with another will give inspiration and create compassionate bonding.

It will be a time in which being emotionally vulnerable is "in" and supported. Corporations, businesses, and schools will have Emotional Healing (EH) rooms available to workers anytime they have an emotional reaction they want to process. In the room, the walls and floor will be padded with six inch thick, soft-enough-for-pounding but durable fabric. There will be big pillows to cuddle up in or pound on, life-size dolls of a man, a woman, and a male and female child. There will also be towels for biting and twisting and foam bats for pounding.

Tomorrow morning arise and through a portal in time— see a local factory worker being upset by her foreman looking over her shoulder. She is nervous and her hands break out into a cold sweat. She goes to the Emotional Healing Room. In the E.H. room she confronts a man size rag-type doll using her physical symptoms as her springboard into what she is feeling about this man. After using the formula described in chapter six, Dehila discovers that she was molested beginning at age two. This knowledge comes to her on an emotional level. Her body physically reacts verifying the memory. It is not something she intellectually knew, but her body's cellular memory recorded the age two trauma and she now finds herself squatting in the corner of the E.R. room sucking her thumb and scared. She begins to tremble:

The E.H. room momentarily takes on the image of her childhood bedroom. She forces herself to ask the questions, "Where am I? How old am I? Who is with me? What is happening? How do I feel?" She pays attention to her body sensations and gestures as she asks these questions.

Dehlia feels her body-mind becoming two years old again. Her muscles go weak and she feels like she is slumping into motionlessness and powerlessness, perhaps fainting. She hears herself crying, "No daddy, no daddy." The man size rag doll falls on her as she sits in the corner. In her two year old state of mind, she is unable to push it off.

At this point in this hypothetical E.H. experience, Dehlia may want to call in a peer counselor, or the staff Body-mind expert. (Counseling psychologists, psychiatrists, and psychotherapists who are well versed in the physical and bio-electromagnetic aspects of emotional processing are now called Body-mind experts.) When one is in the depths of emotionally healing wounds from the past, it is easier to have another person do the head work so full attention can be given to feeling the feelings to completion. A buzzer is within Dehlia's reach to signal her desire for a counselor/coach to travel this inward journey with her. She pushes it and within two minutes a peer counselor, selected ahead of time by Dehlia, walks in and joins her in the corner. The healing process, as described earlier, is taken to completion.

There is no time limit and no pay cut for the time spent processing and healing. In actuality, far less time is lost per employee per year since this program began 18 months ago. Instead of weeks or months lost, in the past, due to illness, nervous breakdowns, and drug rehabilitation, a few hours and a day now and then are the usual limits of time taken by employees. There is so much loving support to process emotions and own feelings in the work place that blame, judgement of any kind, racism, sexism, and dishonesty are almost non-existent. When there is a flare up it is immediately recognized as a symptom of a hurt child-self and an E.H. room is sought to process and heal the wound. Within this kind of atmosphere people want to go to work everyday. The rewards are not only financial, but also emotional and spiritual, leaving the individual feeling whole and, most importantly, loved and worthwhile.

The entire educational system is being revised. From kindergarten on through graduation, people are encouraged to do what they like to do because educators know it is in their likes that their students talents lie. There is an underlying trust that enough people like to dig ditches, enough people like to be plumbers, teachers, child care givers, etc., etc.

One required subject throughout the schooling years is the study of "Being Who You Naturally Are" and the studying of all life, without dissection, "Being Who And What It Naturally Is". Humans are learning about other species through the use of telepathy, clair-sentience, and other metaphysical, non-intrusive and non-violent means. This kind of sensitivity training teaches the at-one-ment of humans with all other species.[1]

This training and way of learning are being implemented worldwide. Part of the training includes the emotional-unfinished-business house cleaning going on at work, school and in all institutions. As a person gets free of cumbersome emotional baggage, the spiritual sensitivity increases. A cross section of spiritual practices are offered to students at school and adults at work. Patriarchal religions and practices such as Christianity, Buddhism, Judaism, Hinduism, Islam, Sufism, Taoism, etc., have all evolved and updated their language and history to demonstrate the importance of both sexes in their religions. Women have always played equally important roles in religion. They simply were not recognized. As a result, all spiritual and emotional lessons in all religions now require the development of both the feminine and the masculine aspects of all human beings.

In schools and businesses specific religions are not taught. But, the spiritually balancing aspects such as use of breath, active and passive meditation techniques, relaxation techniques, chakra balancing methods, the importance of music, use of the imagination and dream interpretation are offered in the public sector. Teaching of spiritual practices along with emotional healing methods have fostered respect for differences. Worship of the Goddess is as revered as worship of God. No religious practice proclaims to have the one and only way to worship. The discovery that addictions, child abuse, spouse abuse, and drug abuse were symptoms of unfinished emotional business, lack of self-worth, and spiritual hunger resulted in these world-wide programs being implemented in schools and businesses.

To see what the effects of these programs are going to have on the world, let us take our magical fantasy seven years into the future: Year 2000:

Since sensations of judgement, blame, and acting out of pent up emotions are now immediately seen as signs of a need to process feelings and heal child-self wounds, the majority of people immediately seek an EH room. They are as prevalent and accessible as bathrooms. Even a person walking down the street can step into a publicly provided facility. E.H. rooms, coupled with whole person counseling centers, have virtually replaced police stations and are modeled after the Japanese idea of a police station on every block. Only now they are called Emotional Healing Centers which most people call "EH rooms". It is as acceptable for a teenager to excuse himself to go to an EH room as it is to go to the bathroom.

There are gun and ammunition recycle stations temporarily set up to handle the number of different weapons being discarded. No one kills animals unless it is directly for food. Those who kill animals now do so after much psycho-spiritual and physical "how to" training. Killing of wild animals for food is done only in places where domestically raised food is not available. In the United States

130

hunting has virtually stopped. The awakening of the importance of all emotions led hunters everywhere to remember how awful and often sick they felt at their first kill, which usually occurred around age ten. After awakening and healing that memory, they no longer wanted to kill because they no longer had to do it in order to get dad's "love" and approval, nor to be manly.

Meat, fish, and poultry are still available but in greatly reduced quantities. The awakening of the emotions has resulted in people also *feeling* their physical bodies and they realize that at the most, one serving of animal, fish or fowl protein a week is plenty. Most have changed to eating it only once a month, having decided to get their protein from grains and legumes. And many people have animal flesh protein only on very special occasions. Consequently, the mass raising of beef and hogs was found unnecessary and the lessened kill afforded a more naturally reverent form of killing of all animal food along with extra time to focus on raising mineralized, toxin free environmentally compatible beef, poultry, pork, fish, grains, vegetables and fruits.

The vast amount of land that was used to feed all the food animals now raises enough grains, legumes, vegetables, and fruits to feed all the people on planet Earth. The rain forests are no longer being destroyed but being restored. As a result, the increased vegetation and trees are providing enough oxygen to counteract the, much feared in the 80's, Green House effect. An environmentally conscious and loving technology and industry has also contributed to stopping the air, land, and water pollution. A man or woman living in at-one-ment with Nature can no longer consciously destroy it.

The over population of the human species peaked in the mid 1990's. As deep awareness of our sacred interaction with all other species developed, the global birth rate sharply declined as we sought ways to balance our numbers with all of the other species. Women and men who choose not to have children and those who could not, realized their life's purpose and energy was to be focused on other altruistic endeavors.

Homosexuality became accepted and understood to be Nature's way of helping to curb over population. Other species have been an example of this down through the centuries. Ducks, geese, wolves and other animals in direct correlation, have more incidence of same sex relationships when food supply is not plentiful.

As the balance in Nature begins to restore itself, cross-species communication increases. Much is being learned from other animals, plants, and minerals. Like two races of people intermingling to develop understanding and appreciation for each other's uniqueness, humans are developing a friendship and sense of community with all other species on planet Earth.

With the education of the equality of the feminine and masculine aspects in each human being, it is being realized that bisexuality is actually the most psychologically healthy state of mind. This is resulting in teenage same sex, affectionate relationships (but not necessarily sexual) naturally increasing to well over 50%, again, a natural way of preventing pregnancies, but also a nurturing, loving way for each teenager to learn self-respect and self-esteem prior to adulthood.

These relationships are teaching that friendship is the true basis for any form of bonding, whether with the same sex or with the opposite sex. Emphasis on friendship and creative development of abilities and likes is prevalent in the 20 year olds. Among the thirty year olds, there are about 50% in heterosexual relationships in the United States today (year 2000). Even though these are now the child bearing years, less than 50% of the couples are having children—a natural and happy response of both child rearing and non-child rearing couples to the over population problem.

The healing of the child-self has virtually stopped adults from having children through which they vicariously live. Adults are now living happy and creatively stimulated lives eliminating the desire to have a child do it for them. Thus, this form of child abuse is practically extinct.

A research breakthrough in 1995, on death and life beyond the grave, proved without a shadow of doubt that consciousness does not die when the body does, nor is consciousness killed by abortion. Advanced technology in the use of low frequency—high amplitude sound waves was used to communicate with people after their death and with consciousness before birth.[2] In the two years since the confirmation, people have been re-educating themselves about their bio-spiritual purposes. No longer is death feared. This has resulted in an education program titled, "Transitioning with Dignity". It is taught to all ages and especially the terminally ill.

It is realized that we all choose how we will die.[3] Violent deaths have reduced considerably, in number, as a result of this knowledge. Still, most of us hide the knowledge from ourselves so we can more fully focus on living.

When the time comes the preparation for death has become a special ceremony and a grieving yet happy time much like a going away party. Children especially enjoy the new attitude about death. They feel much freer to express their views from a position of childlike wonder as they are dying. Children are, in fact, teaching the adults of the old system how to "die with dignity".

This new attitude about death is turning the mass consciousness around 180 degrees regarding the use of medicines to cure diseases. We now understand that illnesses such as colds and flu, etc., are ways the immune system gives itself a workout.

It was discovered that antibiotics, cold suppressants, and pain relievers actually interfered with the duties and abilities of the immune system. They discovered that the over use of antibiotics back in the 50's, 60's, 70's and 80's resulted in a major genetic breakdown of the immune system leading to a disease called AIDS.

We now know that AIDS, cancer, and other potentially fatal diseases are also Nature's way of correcting our disconnect from our natural selves. We accept these ways of correction on the unconscious level so that we can stay focused on feeling physically alive. Some people, it is now accepted, enjoy struggling with the elements. The struggle makes them feel more alive. Because of this general knowledge, the *choices* of diseases, accidents, etc., of individuals are more accepted and respected than ever before.

Because more and more people are consciously creating their reality, surgeries and transplants are down 70%. People are less and less afraid to die and more and more are enjoying their awakened creativity. As their child-selves healed so did their aches and pains, freeing them to more fully experience biological spirituality.

Quality play time for the inner child-self awakened naturalists to the fact that it isn't survival of the fittest that other species have been trying to exemplify but a *quality* of life and natural state of grace.

*Just imagine what quality your life would have if
all feelings were owned and processed.*

*Just imagine if all fears, except the two natural
ones of falling and loud noises, were gone because
there was no more crime.*

*Just imagine what a world would be like if you
knew your individual way would be respected and
individual honesty and integrity were such a
natural way of living that you could trust everyone
to be practicing them.*

*Just imagine being here on Earth to fulfill your
talents to their fullest and in doing so you filled
yourself and the world with an indescribable love
and joy of creativity.*

Just imagine...

Imagine

Chapter Eleven Notes

1. Research in the fields of telepathy, clairsentience, psychokinesis, etc., has been being impeccably, scientifically conducted for the past 100 years. The International Institute of Integral Studies has two of these top scientists on staff, Dr. Bernard Grad, and Dr. Douglas Dean. For more information about the research going on world wide contact I.I.I.H.S. at P.O.Box 1387, Stn. H; Montreal, Quebec H3G 2N3.

2. Research about life after death has been going on in several countries. The United States acknowledges it the least, Eastern European countries and Great Britain acknowledge it the most. At the library look it up under "Psychical Research." There is plenty of evidence proving communication with the deceased is possible.

3. Roberts, Jane, *The Nature Of Personal Reality*. Read Seth session 665 for more information about this.

I AM governing vessel. I govern the flow of your love,

compassion and creativity by tuning into and responding to your beliefs. What you believe I direct energy toward manifesting.

I am stomach, small intestine, gall bladder, bladder, large intestine and the heat energy in your body. I ingest, process, distribute, store and eliminate with the help of the heat energy available to me.

I am the backbone of your being. I cradle your creativity. I put your ideas and imaginings into action. I dance with your vision of tomorrow and make it what you believe it will be.

And when you are ready to go beyond I am there ready to take you. I am your Brahman's gate to your Soul and All-That-Is.

Affirmation:
I am the electrical charge
that unites with your magnetic substance
self forming the marriage of Spirit with Form.
I am more than my body even while my form is
as divine as my spirit. My form is my spirit
made manifest and I am born
naturally good.

✳

Appendix One
Volitional Trip Into Spirit World

In 1978 my father died. He and I had been very close and I deeply grieved his passing. It was as though my very reason for living had been taken away from me. I so longed for him to resurrect from the dead, or for me to die, that I began hearing voices, had lucid dreams, and finally had an out of body trip to spirit world similar to those of core near death experiencers. It was the visit to my father in the spirit world that set me on a full time quest to learn about these inner experiences. It happened while I was receiving an eclectic style massage. I was a student of yoga and had learned to use a very relaxing form of breathing called the ujjayi breath. I began doing this style of deep breathing as soon as I got on the massage table. Within minutes I began to lose sensation of the massage therapist touching my body, yet, I could see where she was working on me even though I had my eyes shut. When she placed her hands on my abdomen a shaft of royal purple light shot out of my navel. It rose about eighteen inches in the air and was about four inches in diameter. I tried to sit up but couldn't. For some reason it was instantly okay that I couldn't.

That feeling of okay signaled the experience to continue. A black void briefly engulfed me. Then a huge eye appeared to be looking at me. It soon disappeared being replaced by a baby's face charred with gaping cuts, as if the flesh was falling off the cheeks and forehead. The oldest child, my sister Marilyn, was badly burned at age six. A month later, a few days before her seventh birthday, she had died. I wondered whether the face was hers or if it was a symbol of me and my grief? I didn't get an answer. Instead, a kaleidoscope of brilliant colors flashed before my eyes. At the moment of seeing such brilliant colors, I realized I must be somewhere other than in the physical world. I had no particular belief about life after death but I thought, "If I am in a world that happens after death maybe I could see my father." I mentally asked to see him and he appeared, smiling, standing under what looked like an overgrown bonsai bush.

Dad looked to be in his late thirties, which would have been his age when I was conceived. Without using words, I communicated, "But, you were seventy-two when you died." As I had this thought he simultaneously changed into the image of himself in his seventies. Then it occurred to me that he was no longer even physical; what did he look like now? I felt him laugh at my never ending curiosity. As a child I was one of those tireless pests that asked questions for which there were no answers. I felt his love come through his laugh at the active child still very much alive in me. With the request to see what he looked like now, I experienced a falling sensation, like the start one experiences when falling out of bed and suddenly waking up. Instead of awakening, however, I arrived at a still lake, nestled between very tall mountain ranges. In the distance I saw a light. It drew closer until it became like a moon of pulsating white light hovering over the lake. A "knowing" came to me that this was the end of my journey to a place where the worlds of the seen and the unseen can meet when the desire or need is strong enough.

I will never forget the rhythm of that pulsating, white light. I carry it with me always. During the massage my body temperature had dropped so far that I needed help getting off the table and walking. After one-half hour I was still deeply entranced and barely able to walk. The massage therapist drove me home. In seventy degree weather I climbed into bed, turned the electric blanket on high, and slept without moving for twelve hours. I awoke in the same position and spot in bed that I had fallen asleep. No drugs or alcohol had been taken prior to this experience.

Appendix Two
EMOTIONAL ENERGY DEVELOPMENT CHART
EXPANDED

This is an expansion of the Emotional Energy Development Chart on pages 18 & 19. It describes the possible spiritual/emotional wound and its symptoms in each age of development.

AGE: Infancy.(conception through nine months) the "I am you" stage.

WOUND: Spirit has difficulty becoming one with flesh due to either the child not wanting to be born, or either of the parents not wanting the child.

SYMPTOMS:

- Difficulty being born, such as premature birth and at-birth complications.

- Early childhood life-threatening diseases.

- Oral addictions: food, drink (caffeine & alcohol), drugs (over the counter & prescription), sex.

- Seldom, if ever, feels "good" enough.

- Disassociates feeling from the body, and thoughts from feelings.

- Is insecure emotionally and physically.

- Goes to lots of doctors and/or therapists and nothing seems to work.

WAYS TO HEAL:

- Water rebirthing

- Warm to hot baths

- Nurturing safe bodywork

- Allow yourself to be rocked and to feel loved unconditionally.

- Give all of your wounded feelings to a doll and hold and rock him or her. Do this daily.

AGE: Pre-toddler (9 months to 18 months), the "I am you and me" stage.

WOUND: The pattern of the wounds of the parents becomes adapted and lays the foundation for the wounds of the child.

SYMPTOMS:

- Disconnected from feelings

- Disconnected from compassion for others and other species

- Disconnected from childlike wonder and play

- Disconnected from nurturing and compassionate, i.e., "feminine" self.

- Having children because you want someone to love you

- Child abuse

- Having unwanted children

- Spouse abuse

- Animal abuse

- Condones physical violence such as war, corporal punishment, capital punishment, and, trophy or "sport" hunting.

WAYS TO HEAL:

- Loving bonding experiences such as with a life long friend, other species, companions, etc.

- At-one with nature experiences such as provided by vision quests, outward bound programs, nature walks.

- Healing the Inner Child and Awakening the Wonder Child programs—making the healing and awakening a way of life.

AGE: Toddler (18 months to 3 years) the "I am me" stage.

WOUND: Being forced to act like your parents want you to act instead of being encouraged to feel your feelings and to be who you naturally are.

SYMPTOMS:

- Either overly compliant or overly rebellious
- Either indecisive or compulsive
- Stuck in false guilt or easily feeling ashamed
- Either very soft-spoken or booms in a loud voice
- Sees things in terms of either-or, black or white, right or wrong.

WAYS TO HEAL:

- Learn to say "No" without guilt
- Learn to express mountains of repressed anger to *completion.*
- Learn the connection between being able to express anger and your emotional boundaries.
- Honor your likes and preferences.

AGE: *Preschool (Age 3 through 5, or until second teeth come in) the independent stage*

WOUND: Contaminated decisions about life: If a person doesn't feel unconditionally loved, free to love self and other, and encouraged to Be, decisions about what life is are made based upon these wounds and have long term effects on our relationships with others.

SYMPTOMS:

- Difficulty having loving and cooperative relationships with others
- Emotional boundary issues—has trouble knowing what are her/his feelings and what are other's feelings.
- Makes guesses and assumptions based on fears and the disconnection between feelings and thoughts.
- Does not emotionally know oneself, therefore cannot easily trust intuitions and gut feelings.
- Discounts feelings, over rationalizes.
- Eventually develops digestive and/or heart related problems.

AGE: *School age (Age 6 through 12 approximately) the interdependent stage.*

WOUND: Not feeling "good enough" just the way you are.

SYMPTOMS:

- Prejudging and degrading of others.

- Competitive against others

- Or, is withdrawn and feels like a victim.

- Uncomfortable in social situations, and /or is more comfortable with one sex than the other.

WAYS TO HEAL:

- Men's bonding groups for men, women's bonding groups for women.

- Heal the first three chakras and grieve the losses of your childself.

- Change the internal critical parent voice to one of nurturing and unconditional love.

- Join groups that are based on cooperation.

The first five stages culminate into the next two. All stages are continuously interacting. These last two stages describe the possibilities if the first five functioning.

AGE: *Adolescence*

POSSIBILITIES: If emotional energies (Chakras 1-5) are happily functioning, adolescence has the potential of being a time of awakening the psychospiritual skills essential to experience awe and wonder in one's life.

AWE AND WONDER SKILLS:

- Respect and appreciation for differences.

- Is naturally loving, know own emotional boundaries and feels free and safe to share feelings, ideas and dreams.

- Sees and experiences feminine aspects, masculine aspects and Childlike wonder with equal importance.

- Creative energies abound and there is unlimited opportunity coming from the happy adult world to pursue them. Every day is a whole new world to explore and enjoy.

METHODS OF AWAKENING:

- Family/community ceremonies celebrating the rites of passage of childhood Development stages; adolescence into womanhood and manhood.

- School and community fostered classes on developing psychospiritual daily habits/practices such as breathing and Healing the Inner Child techniques for emotional/physical and spiritual health, and games and activities that foster cooperation, not competition.

- Classes and activities that promote the likes and preferences of the students and that fosters the use of these likes into ways to make a living or career direction.

- A massive global consciousness that believes emotions are equal in importance to intellect, the feminine is equal in importance to the masculine, and that quality of life of other species is equally important to the quality of life of the human species.

AGE: Adult (Self-actualized age)

POSSIBILITIES: A self-actualized person is one who feels, deals and heals feelings, follows her/his bliss and is continually fulfilling his/her loving creative desires. S/he exudes an inner peace (not complacency) and an enthusiasm/passion for daily living. Doing seemingly mundane daily chores can be a bliss-filled experience for this person. There is often an aura of reverence for all life about her/him.

SYMPTOMS OF REVERENCE: "Symptoms of Inner Peace," from an anonymous source expresses the symptoms of reverence:

SYMPTOMS OF INNER PEACE

Watch for signs of Peace. The hearts of a great many have already been exposed to it and it seems likely that we could find our society experiencing it in epidemic proportions.

Some signs and symptoms of inner peace:

✧ *Tendency to think and act spontaneously rather than from fear.*

✧ *An unmistakable ability to enjoy each moment.*

✧ *Loss of interest in judging other people.*

✧ *Loss of interest in judging self.*

✧ *Loss of interest in interpreting the actions of others.*

✧ *Loss of interest in conflict.*

✧ *Loss of ability to worry (a very serious symptom).*

✧ *Frequent, overwhelming episodes of appreciation.*

✧ *Contended feelings of connectedness with others and with nature.*

✧ *Frequent attacks of smiling through the eyes and from the heart.*

✧ *Increasing tendency to let things happen rather than make them happen.*

✧ *Increased susceptibility to Love extended by others as well as the uncontrollable urge to extend it.*

If you have all or even most of the above symptoms, please be advised that your condition may be too far advanced to turn back. If you are exposed to anyone exhibiting several of these symptoms, remain exposed at your own risk. The condition of Inner Peace is likely well into its infectious stage. Be forewarned.

Appendix Three
RESOURCES

For healing the inner child via acupressure:

Hummingbird Home
P.O. Box 57
Conklin, MI 49403
616-677-2765
Director: Nancy Fallon, PhD., C.I. for AOBTA
Offering: Shin Shiatsu
             Biological Spirituality
             Awakening the Wonder Child

Jin Shin Do Bodymind Acupressure
366 California Ave. #16
Palo Alto, California 94306
415-328-1811
Director: Iona Marsaa Teeguarden, M.T., M.A., M.F.C.C.
Offering: Bodymind Psychotherapy

For various forms of Shiatsu bodywork:

Ohashiatsu Institute
12 West 27th
New York, New York 10001
212-684-4190
Offering: World wide training in highly acclaimed *Ohashiatsu*

American Oriental Bodywork Therapy Association
(AOBTA)
6801 Jericho Tpk.
Syossett, New York 11791
516-364-5533
Offering: Information on Nationally & Internationally Registered
             Therapists of the various forms of Shiatsu.

For college degree information about body, mind, spirit studies:

The International College of Spiritual & Psychic Sciences
P.O. Box 1445, Station H
Montreal, Quebec H3G 2N3
Offering: Seminary degrees and certificates.
ICSPS is dedicated to human psychophysical integration and
psychospiritual awareness. President: Rev. Marilyn Zwaig Rossner, PhD.,
Ed.D.

Medicina Alternativa Institute
Affiliated to the Open International University
28, International Buddhist Centre Road,
Colombo 6, Sri Lanka
Telex: 23039 LINK CE, or Fax: 0094-1-584148

Offering: Bachelor through Doctorate degrees in Traditional
            and Alternative Medicine. Medicina Alternative
            Institute has branches and affiliated associations
            throughout the World.

For Seth groups and classes available nationally and internationally
            contact:
            Seth Network International
            P.O. Box 1620
            Eugene, OR 97440-1620
            USA

Bibliography

An Outline of Chinese Acupuncture. China, Peking: Foreign Languages Press. 1975.

Atwater, P.M.H. *Coming Back To Life.* New York: Dodd, Mead & Company. 1988.

Bentov, Itzak. *Stalking The Wild Pendulum.* Rochester, Vermont, Destiny Books. 1977 by Itzak Bentov, 1988 by Mirtala Bentov.

Bradshaw, John. *The Family, A Revolutionary Way of Self Discovery.* Deerfield Beach, Florida: Health Communications, Inc. 1988.

. *Homecoming, Reclaiming and Championing Your Inner Child.* New York: Bantam Books. 1990.

. *Creating Love, The Next Great Stage of Growth.* New York: Bantam Books. 1992.

Campbell, Joseph with Moyers, Bill, Flowers, Betty Sue, Ed. *The Power of Myth,* New York: Doubleday. 1988.

Connelly, Dianne, PhD. (1979) *Traditional Acupuncture: The Law of the Five Elements.* Maryland, Columbia: The Centre for Traditional Acupuncture Inc., 1975.

Crim, Keith, Ed. (1988) *The Perennial Dictionary of World Religions.* Originally published under the title, *Abingdon Dictionary of Living Religions.* Abingdon Press. San Francisco: Harper & Row. 1981.

Ferguson, Marilyn. *The Aquarian Conspiracy.* Los Angeles: J.P. Tarcher, Inc. 1980.

Fox, Matthew. *A Spirituality Named Compassion.* San Francisco: Harper. 1979. 1990.

Inglis, Brian, ed., *Mediumship and Survival.* London: Paladin Books. 1982.

. *Hauntings and Apparitions, An Investigation of the Evidence.* London: Granada Publishing. 1982 by Andrew MacKenzie.

. *Through the Time Barrier.* London: Paladin Books. 1983 by Danah Zohar.

Kalweit, Holger. *Dreamtime and Inner Space: The World of the Shaman.*

. *Shamans, Healers, and Medicine Men.* Boston: Shambhala. 1992.

Kubler-Ross, Elizabeth, M.D. *On Death and Dying.* New York: Macmillan Publishing Co. Inc. 1969. Thirteenth printing, 1978.

. *Death, The Final Stage of Growth.* Englewood Cliffs, New Jersey: Prentice Hall. 1975.

Kushi, Michio. *How to See Your Health: Book of Oriental Diagnosis.* Tokyo: Japan Publications. 1980.

Leonard, George. *The Silent Pulse.* New York: Elsevier-Dutton Publishing Co, Inc., 1978. Reprinted by Bantam Books, 1981.

Mayer, Robert. *Through Divided Minds, Probing the Mysteries of Multiple Personalities.* New York: Avon Books. 1988.

Masunaga, Shizuto with Wataru Ohashi. *Zen Shiatsu.* Tokyo: Japan Publications. 1977.

Meek, George, Ed. *Healers and the Healing Process.* Wheaton, IL: Theosophical Publishing House, 1977; third printing. 1982.

Moody, Raymond, Jr., M.D. *Life After Life & Reflections on Life After Life.* New York: Guideposts. 1975.

Motoyama, Hiroshi. *Theories of the Chakras: Bridge to Higher Consciousness.* Wheaton, IL: The Theosophical Publishing House, 1981. Second Printing. 1984.

Ohashi, Wataru. *Touching The Invisible, An Introduction To Oriental Diagnosis.* New York: Ohashi Institute. 1985.

Reich, Wilhelm. (1973, by Mary Boyd) *Selected Writings.* New York: Farrar, Straus and Giroux, 1951.

Ring, Kenneth. *Heading Toward Omega.* New York: William Morrow and Co., Inc. 1984.

Roberts, Jane. *The Coming of Seth.* New York: Frederick Fell Publishers, Inc. 1966.

. *The Seth Material.* Englewood Cliffs, NJ: Prentice-Hall, Inc. 1970.

. *Seth Speaks.* Englewood Cliffs, NJ: Prentice-Hall, Inc. 1972.

. *The Nature of Personal Reality: A Seth* Book. Englewood Cliffs, NJ: Prentice-Hall, Inc. 1974.

. *The Nature of the Psyche: Its Human* Expression. Englewood Cliffs, NJ: Prentice-Hall, Inc. 1979.

. *The "Unknown" Reality, Vol. I & II.* Englewood Cliffs, NJ: Prentice-Hall, Inc. 1979.

. *The Individual and the Nature of Mass* Events. Englewood Cliffs, NJ: Prentice-Hall, Inc. 1981.

. *The God of Jane: A Psychic Manifesto.* Englewood Cliffs, NJ: Prentice-Hall, Inc. 1981.

. *Dreams, "Evolution," and Value* Fulfillment, Vol. I & II New York: Prentice-Hall, Inc. 1986.

. *Seth. Dreams and Projection of* Consciousness. Walpole, NH: Stillpoint Publishing. 1986.

Roberts, Jane and Butts, Robert. Seth Class Notes. Unpublished.

Schaef, Ann Wilson. *Co-Dependence.* Minneapolis: Winston Press. 1986.

. *When Society Becomes An Addict.* San Francisco: Harper & Row, Publishers. 1987.

Sinetar, Marsha. *Ordinary People as Monks and* Mystics. Mahwah, NJ: Paulist Press. 1986.

Sjoo, Monica and Mor, Barbara. *The Great Cosmic* Mother. San Francisco: Harper & Row. 1987.

Steinem, Gloria. *Revolution From Within.* Boston: Little Brown, & Co. 1992, 1993.

Steiner, Claude. *Scripts People Live.* New York: Grove Press, Inc. 1974.

Stone, Merlin. *When God Was A Woman.* Harvest/HBJ edition Dial Press. New York. 1976.

Teaguarden, Iona. *Acupressure Way to Health: Jin Shin Do.* Tokyo: Japan Publications. 1978.

von Heydebrand, Caroline. *Childhood: A Study of the Growing Child.* Translated by Daphne Harwood. Hudson, New York: Anthroposophic Press. 1988.

Wegscheider-Cruse, Sharon. *Another Chance, Hope and Health for the Alcoholic Family.* Palo Alto, CA: Science and Behavior Books, Inc. 1981.

. *The Miracle of Recovery.* Deerfield Beach, FL: Health Communications, Inc. 1989.

Watkins, Sue. *Conversations with Seth, Vol. I & II.* Englewood Cliffs, NJ: Prentice-Hall, Inc. 1980.

Xinnong, Cheng, chief editor. *Chinese Acupuncture and Moxibustion.* Beijing: Foreign Languages Press. 1987.

Zukav, Gary. *The Dancing Wu Li Masters* New York: William Morrow and Co., Inc. 1979.